ECD
30 Years of Energy Conscious Design

Contents

Dedicated to **Dominic Michaelis**
Solar Architect and Inventor

Foreword

Paul Morrell

About 15 years ago, just halfway through the life of ECD, I sat with two different architectural practices that had been approached to consider a new, economic approach to low energy housing. Each opened the meeting by saying to me, "Don't say it can't be all glass," to which I replied: "It can't be all glass." We didn't get on.

This may have been nothing more than a failure of imagination on my part, but I prefer to think of it as evidence of a perfectly human tendency, when faced with change, to try and carry on much as before. It is so much easier to carry forward the old thinking, good as it may be, and then just add stuff to meet the new situation. But it is also wasteful and, at its worst, leads to Frankenstein architecture.

We therefore owe a lot to those who go straight to new thinking, who recognise that the implications of that new situation run so deep that there is a need to go back to first principles, to research and to experiment. There were not many who did, and fewer still who have held a steady course through the journey described in this book: broadly a decade of lonely pioneering, followed by a decade of campaigning with like minds, and finally a decade of being joined by the mainstream.

Along the way, the concept of 'sustainability' often became confused, so that the sponsors of any building that had a bird box and a bike shelter laid claim to the title. Now, if we know anything, we know that it is fundamentally about energy — so how prescient it was to have christened a practice Energy Conscious Design at the very beginning of that journey.

So all strength to ECD, and here's to another 10 years of lighting the way.

Paul Morrell
Government Chief Construction Adviser

Introduction
by David Turrent and Richard Ferraro

This book describes ECD's output of specialised work over the past 30 years, from 1980 to the present day. We have structured the material into three main chapters, one for each decade, each with a selection of featured projects. For each decade we have reviewed the work in the wider context of sustainable architecture and the prevailing economic circumstances. We have also tried to give a flavour of the wider attitudes to sustainability and in particular the legislative framework applicable at the time.

The 1980s was, for us, a period of research and experimentation. We definitely felt like pioneers, working in uncharted territory and on the fringes of conventional architectural practice. In the 'green' '90s, we enjoyed a significant increase in workload and expanded our activities from mainly residential to larger, non-domestic projects. The focus in this period shifted from 'energy' to a wider sustainability agenda. It was a very creative and productive time for ECD, which saw the completion of a number of cutting-edge projects. Climate change emerged as the key topic in the 'noughties', together with a proliferation of design guidelines and new performance standards — including legally binding targets for CO_2 reduction and a road map to 'zero carbon' buildings within the next decade.

By 2007, sustainability had become mainstream in terms of architectural practice, and ECD continued to contribute exemplar projects to an emerging body of 'sustainable' architecture in the UK. In 2010 we are focusing on the challenges of upgrading the existing housing stock, and on designing sustainable schools, communities and industries. In the future, there will be huge demands on the architectural profession to deliver low and zero carbon buildings. This, however, is the story of the pioneering years of our practice, Energy Conscious Design, which nailed its colours to the mast and set sail one sunny day in 1980.

In fact, the two of us first met in 1973 as architectural students in the office of Dominic Michaelis Associates, which was then based in a warehouse at Paddington Basin in west London. In those days the Basin was near derelict, home to Westminster's dustcarts and archaic canal dwellers

Prototype solar powered hot-air balloon, comprising a thin transparent outer skin and a black inner trefoil lining to absorb solar radiation. Dominic Michaelis (assisted by David Turrent), 1972.

Solar house at Rustrel, France.
Dominic Michaelis, 1969.

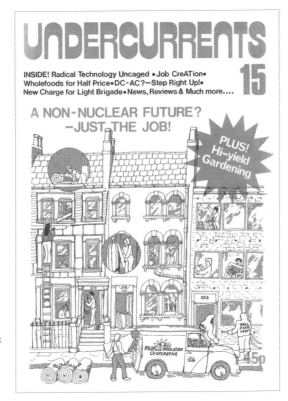

Issue 15 of the *Undercurrents* magazine, in 1976, focused on low energy retrofit. *Plus ça change!*

buildings in the UK, Solar Court in Milton Keynes.

In 1973/74 the price of oil quadrupled to nearly $12 per barrel, creating the first real 'carbon crisis' – a clear warning of the fragile nature of our society's dependency on the high consumption of fossil fuels. This was followed, in the UK, by the miners' strike, interrupted power supplies and the three day week. In the office we tried to understand what this meant for the built environment, while writing postgraduate theses on 'Solar Energy in UK Housing' and building Dominic's solar water heaters and balloons in the workshop below the office. In particular, we were interested in developing ways of improving energy efficiency and exploiting the use of solar energy in buildings. Our work extended to developing prototype solar heating components and systems, and measuring their performance in test-rigs and energy efficient buildings.

Following the OPEC oil crisis, Western governments began to wake up (slightly) and wanted to understand what 'alternative energy' could offer. The idea was to reduce dependency on oil and other fossil fuels, for both economic and political benefits. Of course, nobody knew about 'global warming' in those days, or its potentially disastrous effects. In the 1970s, the small group in the UK that was interested in a low carbon future consisted of designers and scientists, enthusiasts and idealists, all committed to the preservation of finite fossil fuel resources and the reduction of global pollution.

living on steam barges. Dominic Michaelis set up his innovative architectural practice there, initially to develop his interest in solar architecture and solar-powered hot air balloons. Together with partners Stephen Szokolay and Roger Francis, Dominic subsequently started a specialist company, Solar Energy Developments, which undertook research and development work alongside built solar projects. These included individual solar houses at Rustrel, Lioux and Toulon in France and, among other

The rear of the solar house at Lioux, designed with small deep-set windows to reduce solar heat gain.

Solar house at Lioux, France, with solar heated water and a solar heated rock store in the basement. A ducted air hypocaust system allows solar energy stored in the rocks to heat the house in cooler periods. Dominic Michaelis and Gilles Bouchez (assisted by Richard Ferraro), 1976.

The bi-monthly magazine, *Undercurrents*, was essential reading if you wanted to keep up with the latest ideas for 'an alternative low energy society' and, of course, the *Whole Earth Catalogue* took pride of place on everyone's bookshelf. Other early influences included the writings of Buckminster Fuller and Reyner Banham's *The Architecture of the Well-tempered Environment.*

The ideas were simple: cut demand for energy, use less oil, gas and coal, and maximise the use of solar, wind, geothermal and other renewable energy sources. The influence of these ideas on how buildings should be designed and the architecture that resulted were significant driving forces in our

work. We realised that proper consideration of how energy was used and conserved in buildings, combined with the desire to maximise use of 'alternative' or 'renewable' forms of energy, all led to changes in the approach to design. These changes included the selection of materials, new construction details and techniques, a different approach to building services, new influences on the internal planning of buildings and climate responsive external design. Add to this a reappraisal of siting, orientation and the relationship between buildings and microclimate, and we had a fair amount to think about!

David worked on developing detailed designs for an Oxford college building (by Oscar Niemeyer and Dominic Michaelis, but unfortunately never built), and we both helped to develop proposals for modular housing systems, and one-off solar houses. Under Dominic's tutelage we became involved in solar research and development work for various industrial companies.

For Richard this included periods in the south of France, building a solar test-rig and supervising construction of Dominic's solar houses at Lioux and Toulon — both of which incorporated air solar collectors and basement thermal rock stores — and an industrial building in Plymouth with solar water heating. These projects involved purpose-built solar components, control systems and air-handling plant, all designed and developed in the Paddington office and manufactured as prototypes.

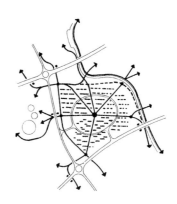

Pennyland, Milton Keynes. Grid square diagram illustrating pedestrian routes.

Pennyland site layout, Milton Keynes. A passive solar layout with most of the houses facing within 30 degrees of due south. John Doggart et al, Milton Keynes Development Corporation, 1977.

At the same time, ECD's third founding partner, John Doggart, was busy in Milton Keynes, working for the Development Corporation and collaborating with Jake Chapman of the Open University. John was trying hard to influence the development of the new town along low energy and solar lines. Several prototype low energy projects were built there at the time, including large-scale field trials of new low energy housing at Pennyland and Great Linford. John and his MKDC colleagues were successful in getting the field trials approved and built, and subsequently in ensuring the energy performance was properly monitored over time by the Open University.

Several of this group of researchers — including Bob Everett, Bob Lowe and Alan Horton — have continued working in low energy housing and renewable energy to this day. In the 1970s and early '80s, however, electronic data recording and computer analysis were in their infancy. To get data for energy consumption and temperatures at the Pennyland field trial, a multitude of meters outside each house had to be read every week for two years. There were large numbers of houses in each experimental group and from this information they plotted the energy savings achieved from the different energy conserving measures.

This work represented some of the best performance data collected in Europe at the time. The results showed the schemes to be cost-effective and encouraged the adoption of low energy housing in Milton Keynes. At the time of writing, in 2010, some of the original research reports* are being made available on the web. Further work by Jake Chapman eventually led to the development of the Milton Keynes Energy Cost Index and, subsequently, Bredem — the Building Research Establishment Domestic Energy Model, which formed the basis for the Standard Assessment

* See *en.wikipedia.org/wiki/Pennyland_project*

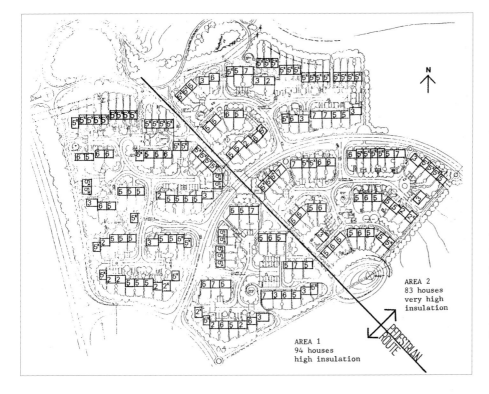

N

AREA 2
83 houses
very high
insulation

AREA 1
94 houses
high insulation

PEDESTRIAN ROUTE

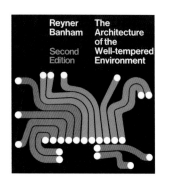

Reyner Banham's *The Architecture of the Well-tempered Environment*, an enduring influence on a whole generation of architects.

Procedure (SAP), updated and still used in 2010 to calculate energy usage in housing.

We met up with John at various conferences on solar energy and low energy housing, and participated in what became the first trade exhibitions of low energy technologies in the UK at *Interbuild* in 1975 and 1977. The 'Ambient Energy Feature' was Dominic Michaelis's idea and design, and the display stands were co-ordinated and built by Richard and a team of architectural students from the UK, France, the USA, Canada and Australia. John represented Milton Keynes as one of a group of exhibitors in the 1975 stand. Like its 1977 counterpart, this was built in bright orange Dexion racking and incorporated whirring wind turbines, solar water heating panels, prototype photovoltaic cells and a variety of insulation products.

David moved on from Dominic's office in the mid-'70s to set up a successful energy research and

Above and right: the Ambient Energy Feature at *Interbuild* in 1977 – one of the earliest displays of low energy technologies in the UK.

development group at the South London Consortium, an architectural practice serving the needs of several inner London local authorities. This allowed him a new platform from which to reach a different audience, and he successfully persuaded various public sector clients to incorporate low energy measures and solar water heating systems into new-build local authority housing schemes. This included a project of his own design in Putney, incorporating one of the first domestic solar water heating systems in the UK. Later in the 1970s, at Stephen George & Partners' London office, David undertook studies on solar-heated houses for the European Commission in Brussels – a very important contact as it turned out.

We had all got to know each other well over seven years. We had exchanged information, knowledge and experience, so it was no surprise when, in 1980, we decided to set up in practice together, with the aim of further developing a design philosophy based on environmental principles.

Our mutual desire was to be masters of our own fate, putting our money where our mouths were by designing and building low energy buildings in what was then (and continued to be for some time) a very niche market. All this was set against a post-war culture of design and development in the UK and Europe that was not much concerned with energy consumption or the conservation of fossil fuels, even though the Western world was then in

Solar water heating system, Putney – one of the first installed in public sector housing in the UK. South London Consortium, 1976.

(including all the 1920s and '30s stock), many of which, in the 1950s and early '60s, were still heated using coal fires. As a result, up to the mid 1960s, there were high levels of atmospheric pollution in the UK and winter 'smog' in the large cities.

Central heating using a single heat source (a boiler) for each dwelling only started to be installed in new housing in the UK in the late 1950s, and it was not until 1965 that thermal performance standards were established within the UK Building Regulations, when U values of 1.7 W/m^2.K were set for external walls and 1.4 for roofs. These standards were tightened in 1976 to 1.0 W/m^2.K for walls and 0.6 for roofs, but single glazing was still the norm in new buildings in the early 1980s, and most domestic boilers were over-sized, with efficiencies of 60 per cent at best.

In 1979, 40 per cent of UK primary energy was used for heating buildings – about half of this for heating houses. It was not until 1985 that thermal standards were further increased (to 0.6 W/m^2.K for external walls and 0.35 for roofs) with a further tightening in 1990 to 0.45 W/m^2.K for walls and 0.25 for roofs.

As the 1980s beckoned, there were signs that attitudes were beginning to change, albeit very slowly. Even so, we never dreamt it would be another 25 years or more before 'energy conscious design' achieved mainstream acceptance.

recession and oil was trading at $35 a barrel – three times higher than after the first oil crisis in 1973/74. With a few notable exceptions architects at this time were, on the whole, obsessed with light and space – a laudable aim, but one which tended to result in large areas of inefficient single glazing and the excessive consumption of energy for space heating and cooling.

In addition, the UK housing stock was characterised by a large number of draughty uninsulated Victorian and early twentieth-century houses

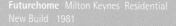

Futurehome Milton Keynes Residential
New Build 1981

Giffard Park Milton Keynes Residential
New Build 1984

Cromartie Road Islington Residential
New Build 1985

Surrey Docks Farm Rotherhithe Agri-
cultural/Residential 1986

Lamerton Street Deptford Residential
New Build 1986

Quantum Centre Hemel Hempstead
Industrial/Offices New Build 1986

Hughes House Milton Keynes Residential New Build 1986

Evelyn Street Deptford Residential
New Build 1987

Spectrum 7 Milton Keynes Industrial
New Build 1987

St Mellons Cardiff Industrial
New Build 1989

Shenley Lodge Milton Keynes Residential New Build 1989

Cromartie Road – Phase 2 Residential
New Build/Refurbishment 1989-93

1980–1990

1 The Pioneering Years

Energy Conscious Design (ECD) was established in May 1980, following the award of a significant contract by the Commission of the European Communities (the CEC, as it was then called). The CEC was setting up a pan-European solar energy research and development programme and we were asked to submit a proposal to co-ordinate a substantial part of it. The application was filled out on David Turrent's kitchen table one evening, having

Commissioned by the CEC, ECD went on to publish 49 *Project Monitors* between 1980 and 1984.

only that afternoon thrashed out the name 'Energy Conscious Design'. There was no formal partnership and we did not have an office or bank account, but these followed swiftly when we heard we had won the contract. Soon after, we moved into our first office in Dryden Street, Covent Garden.

Our task was to appoint and co-ordinate a group of 'experts' within the member states (10 at the time), to investigate and report on the performance of solar heated houses throughout the European Union. One problem to be solved was that different research institutions used different methods of measuring and calculating solar energy contribution, so at the outset we had to reach agreement on a set of standard definitions and methods of measurement. We also developed standard reporting formats for use with both solar water heating systems and solar space heating.

This was interesting work and involved visits to many innovative projects across Europe. We were effectively being paid to learn and the experience provided an ideal base from which to develop a practice combining energy research and consultancy with architecture. It was also a lot of work. The first CEC contract led to the publication of 49 *Project Monitor* brochures describing the design and performance of cutting edge projects within the member states. This was followed by further research work and publications setting out the priorities for future R&D projects, as well as identifying the overall potential for commercial exploitation of solar thermal energy in buildings in Europe.

In the early 1980s there was much interest in the potential of passive solar energy in the UK. 'Passive' systems use normal building elements in a novel way to maximise energy efficiency, while 'active' systems employ mechanical equipment. ECD was commissioned by the Energy Technology Support Unit (ETSU), part of the UK Department of Energy, to investigate the potential for passive solar design in UK housing. The report quantified the energy gains from simple passive features such as

FIG 1. COST / BENEFIT MATRIX FOR NEW-BUILD HOUSING INCORPORATING PASSIVE SOLAR MEASURES

NOTE: Below are summarised the main technical options for passive solar heating. In each box the top figure refers to the extra cost and the bottom figure to the energy saving (kWh/year). Figures below the boxes refer to the residual space heating loads.

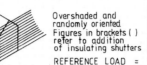
INCREASING THERMAL INSULATION STANDARDS

			1975 BLD. REGS. STANDARD	OVERALL U-VALUE 0·6	OVERALL U-VALUE 0·3 + Double Glazing
BASE		Overshaded and randomly oriented. Figures in brackets ( ) refer to addition of insulating shutters	£0 / 0 kWh	230 / 0·7p/kWh / 3100	640 (1060) / 0·8p/kWh / 6900 (7400)
		REFERENCE LOAD =	12,800 kWh.	9,700	5,900 (5,400)

SIMPLE PASSIVE MEASURES		Correct orientation and minimised overshading	0 / 800	0 / 700	0 / 600
			12,000	9,000	5,300
		Windows re-distributed from north to south elevation.	50 / 0·35p/kWh / 1300	50 / 0·4p/kWh / 1100	50 / 0·5p/kWh / 900
			11,500	8,600	5,000

ADVANCED PASSIVE SOLAR MEASURES		South-facing window area increased to 20 m²	385 / 2.3p/kWh / 1500	340 / 2.8p/kWh / 1300	340 / 2.8p/kWh / 1100
			11,300	8,400	4,800
		Lean-to conservatory covering 10m² of external wall. Figures in brackets ( ) are for a fan assisted system	570 (670) / 1·7p/kWh / 1600 (2200)	570 (670) / 1·9p/kWh / 1400 (1700)	570 (670) / 2·3p/kWh / 1200 (1500)
			11,200 (10,600)	8300 (8000)	4700 (4200)
		20 m² single glazed Trombe wall. Figures in brackets ( ) refer to a double glazed wall.	1000 (1200) / 4·5p/kWh / 2000 (2400)	950 (1150) / 5·3p/kWh / 1600 (2000)	940 (1140) / 6·0p/kWh / 1400 (1800)
			10,800 (10,400)	8100 (7700)	4500 (4100)
		18 m² Roof space collector with fan.	400 / 1·8p/kWh / 2000	400 / 2·3p/kWh / 1600	400 / 3·6p/kWh / 1000
			10,800	8,100	4,900

NOTE: pence per kWh = effective cost of energy assuming a capital repayment factor of 0.09

£270 credit allowed for value of extra space

PASSIVE SOLAR HOUSING IN THE UK

Passive Solar Housing in the UK, a report for the UK Energy Technology Support Unit, published by ECD in 1982.

One of the key diagrams from the report, showing passive solar new-build typologies, with their relative costs and benefits.

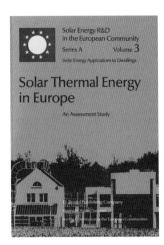

Solar Thermal Energy in Europe, edited by David Turrent and Nick Baker and published by D Reidel in 1983.

A technical study on the potential contribution from solar thermal energy to Europe's energy demand and the report from the first EC Conference on Solar Heating in 1984, the first of many European solar conferences.

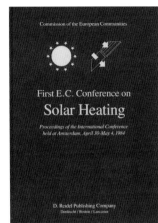

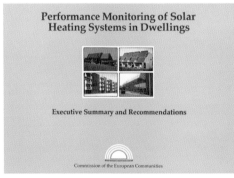

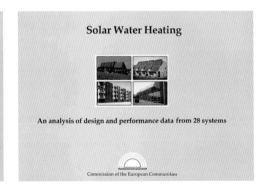

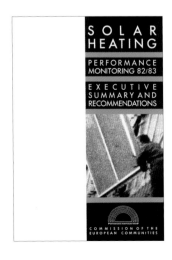

Above and left: the Performance Monitoring Group, part of the CEC Solar Energy R&D programme. Numerous reports were produced by this group of experts from 1982 to '84, summarising the performance of solar heating systems within various European climate zones. Programme and publications co-ordinated by ECD.

Our first computer, an Apple 2 word processor from 1981.

south-facing double-glazed windows and conservatories, as well as demonstrating the implications for site layout and house design. The resulting report, entitled *Passive Solar Housing in the UK*, was hugely influential. We published 1500 copies ourselves and sold them all in less than two years, bar two copies which remain in our office!

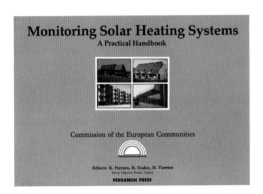

The Earlham Street office in Covent Garden, 1981.

Monitoring Solar Heating Systems, edited by Richard Ferraro, Ramiro Godoy and David Turrent, and published by Pergamon Press in 1983.

These early contracts enabled us to move into larger offices in Earlham Street, Covent Garden. We hired our first employee – a Chilean graduate with a degree in heat transfer physics by the name of Ramiro Godoy, who subsequently went on to enjoy a long career at Max Fordham LLP – and we purchased an Apple 2 word processor together with three pedestal drawing boards. From this base we launched into the search for architectural clients willing to take on our, then, fairly unusual low energy design philosophy, with its emphasis on improving thermal efficiency and utilising passive

A group portrait taken in the Emerald Street office for an article on the practice published by *Building* in April 1984.

Giffard Park, Milton Keynes – passive solar principles applied to a housing scheme for single people.

Above: Lamerton Street, Deptford – co-operative housing in south London, and *(far right)* Cromartie Road, Islington, winner of the RIBA Energy Efficiency Award 1988.

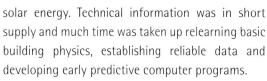

(1976) Building Regulations standard. Windows were double-glazed and a prototype solar water heating system was integrated into the glazed conservatory roof. The main feature of the house was a 'TOTEM' combined heat and power plant (CHP). Based on a Fiat car engine, this generated all of the house's electrical requirements, with the waste heat being used to provide space heating and domestic hot water. Though it was the smallest unit available at the time, it was vastly oversized

solar energy. Technical information was in short supply and much time was taken up relearning basic building physics, establishing reliable data and developing early predictive computer programs.

Our first architectural commission resulted from a call, out of the blue, from the BBC's *Money Programme*, which wanted to do a TV feature on 'the house of the future'. This led, in 1981, to the building of Futurehome 2000 at the Homeworld '81 exhibition in Milton Keynes. Completed in just 12 weeks, the project resulted in a low energy house suitable for mass production, employing a variety of low energy systems.

The house had an L-shaped plan with a south-facing, double-height conservatory occupying the space between the two wings. The design exploited passive solar heat gain in the conservatory, using it to pre-heat incoming fresh air. Construction was in timber frame with thermal insulation standards at twice the then current

for a single dwelling. However, it was an interesting pointer to the future.

The work that followed was mainly carried out for public sector clients, in particular three housing co-operatives that commissioned our first schemes at Giffard Park in Milton Keynes, Cromartie Road in Islington and Lamerton Street in Deptford. Private sector house builders were too busy enjoying the 1980s property boom and had little interest in

Futurehome, Homeworld '81 exhibition, Milton Keynes — an early example of prefabricated timber frame housing in the UK.

The ground and first floor plans of Futurehome, Milton Keynes, showing the relationship of the main living spaces to the conservatory.

Working in the City

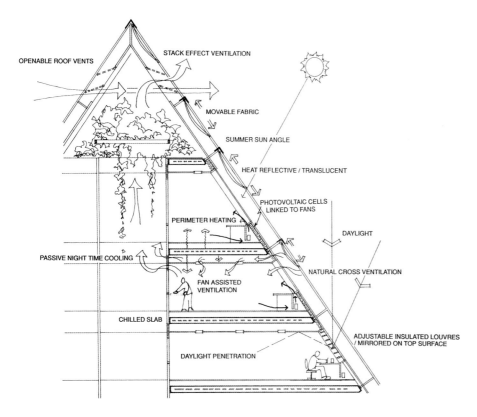

OPENABLE ROOF VENTS

STACK EFFECT VENTILATION

MOVABLE FABRIC

SUMMER SUN ANGLE

HEAT REFLECTIVE / TRANSLUCENT

PHOTOVOLTAIC CELLS LINKED TO FANS

PERIMETER HEATING

DAYLIGHT

PASSIVE NIGHT TIME COOLING

FAN ASSISTED VENTILATION

NATURAL CROSS VENTILATION

CHILLED SLAB

ADJUSTABLE INSULATED LOUVRES / MIRRORED ON TOP SURFACE

DAYLIGHT PENETRATION

Working in the City — ECD's design for a tight urban site showing a double-skin facade and various natural ventilation strategies.

our low energy ideas. Nevertheless, the practice grew rapidly during the 1980s, peaking at around 40 people by the end of the decade, by which time we had moved into new offices in Emerald Street, Holborn, fitted out to our own design.

Several of our early architectural projects were carried out in Milton Keynes, where the Development Corporation was actively promoting energy efficiency by a combination of 'carrot and stick'. The Milton Keynes Energy Park provided us with a number of opportunities, including our competition winning Spectrum 7, a low energy B1 industrial/R&D building that marked our increasing activity as architects in the non-residential commercial sector. In this and in other workplace buildings, and later in educational buildings, we developed a new range of design strategies to keep the sun out, maximise natural daylight, and utilise natural or mechanically assisted ventilation as an alternative to conventional air conditioning.

Winning the competition to build Spectrum 7 wasn't easy, and convincing a pension fund to fund this innovative project proved equally arduous. We were much helped in this by the developer Doug Stewart and the engineers for the project, Bob Emmerson and John Berry of Arup. Bob and John played an unexpected part, as it was the weight of Arup's professional indemnity insurance that reassured the funder regarding the building's innovative services. The project was a success and, in 1989, Spectrum 7 won the Pilkington Award for Low Energy Commercial Buildings of the Year.

Energy consultancy continued to thrive throughout the 1980s, despite cutbacks to R&D programmes imposed by the Thatcher government. This occurred mostly due to the arrival of cheap natural gas in abundance from the North Sea, and the government's belief that nuclear power was the long-term solution to energy supply. ECD's work in this period included the compilation and publication of a *Passive Solar Components Catalogue* and the

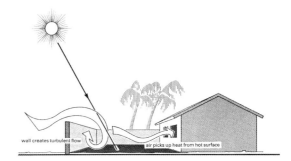

Solar shading and cross-ventilation, just one of the passive cooling design strategies illustrated in the Tropical Island report.

Passive and Low Energy Building Design for Tropical Island Climates, produced for the Commonwealth Science Council in 1987.

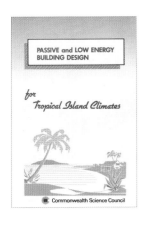

ambitious *Passive Solar Assessment Study*, which calibrated passive solar contributions to heating and cooling in buildings within different climatic zones in Europe. Another key publication was the *Designer's Manual for the Energy Efficient Refurbishment of Housing*, published by the British Standards Institute in 1989 and still relevant today. At this time the Building Research Establishment was responsible for dissemination of low energy design advice through its Best Practice Programme. ECD contributed to this with a number of important research reports, including 'Low Energy Housing at No Extra Cost', 'Energy Efficiency in Schools' and 'Energy Efficiency in Residential Tower Blocks'.

ECD's energy research was not restricted to the UK and Europe, nor wholly limited to work in European climates. The Commonwealth Science Council employed us to conduct workshops in Barbados, which resulted in the publication *Passive and Low Energy Building Design for Tropical Climates*. In the late 1980s we were commissioned with designer

An office visit to Spectrum 7, Milton Keynes, in 1987.

David Graves to design a wind cooled five-star hotel complex in Bonaire, Dutch Antilles, in the trade winds belt off the north coast of Venezuela.

In 1987 David Billingham joined the practice as a partner, providing additional impetus in the public sector, and this resulted in several major estate regeneration projects in Tower Hamlets, Hackney and Kensington in London. These projects were demanding, with extensive resident consultation conducted during the feasibility and design stages. Much of the work involved upgrading inefficient 1960s housing, often deploying external thermal insulation and improved heating systems. These projects also included extensive improvements to security and the quality of the external environment. The work was funded through the government's 'Estate Action' and 'Greenhouse' programmes, the former aimed at improving the existing public sector housing stock and the latter at demonstrating low energy methods of heating for large housing developments. In 1989 we entered another EC design competition, this time for a 'green' office building on a tight urban site in Clerkenwell, and received a Special Mention.

As the 1980s drew to a close, the UK property market crashed. However, we decided to remain optimistic and celebrated our 10th year in practice with an exhibition of our work. We wanted to confirm our core message and the growing validity of that message. We'd done a lot, learned a lot, and we wanted to tell people about it.

Right: site section showing mid-winter sun angles and *(below)*, the south-facing elevation of one of the terraces, showing the lean-to conservatory extensions to the living spaces and their solar water heating systems.

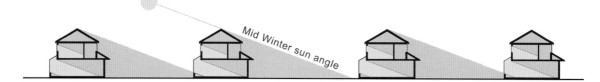

Mid Winter sun angle

South-facing conservatories, with integral solar collectors.

Giffard Park
Milton Keynes 1984

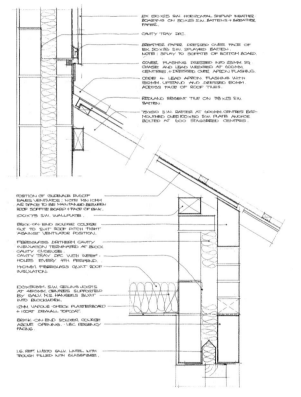

Construction detail showing the fully insulated cavities and lean-to conservatory glazing.

ECD's first public sector housing project was commissioned by the Society for Co-operative Dwellings, an organisation specialising in the housing needs of single people. The Society was keen to build a low energy scheme, as many of their tenants were on low incomes and suffering from fuel poverty. We promoted the scheme as a passive solar demonstration project, which attracted extra grant funding from BRECSU, the Building Research Energy Conservation Support Unit. Meanwhile, the Milton Keynes Development Corporation verified a local need for single-person housing and allocated a site at Giffard Park, adjacent to the Grand Union Canal.

The scheme incorporated 36 flats and shared houses in four south-facing terraces, spaced apart to maximise winter solar gain. South-facing elevations incorporated large double-glazed windows, while windows in north-facing elevations were kept small.

Construction was in loadbearing masonry to maximise thermal mass and, unusually for the time, the 75mm cavities were filled with insulation, resulting in thermal insulation standards far in excess of those specified in the (1976) Building Regulations. Insulated blinds were fitted to the larger south-facing windows, while solar water heating provided pre-heated hot water to the larger dwellings. Space heating was provided by individual gas convectors in each room, and water heating by a small gas circulator serving a hot water cylinder.

Giffard Park was one of a number of European solar projects to be reported within the 'Project Monitor' programme, and detailed performance monitoring showed space heating charges as low as £1 per week, the cost of a pint of beer.

Summer shading of the glazed lean-to conservatory roof.

Cromartie Road

Islington, London   1981

The first phase new-build extension at the eastern end of the Victorian terrace, designed to turn the corner and create a communal south-facing garden.

In 1982 ECD was commissioned by the Islington Community Housing Co-operative to prepare refurbishment proposals for a terrace of Victorian houses along 'energy conscious' lines. A European design competition provided a vehicle to explore the possibility of adding a glazed skin to the rear south elevation, with different modes of operation in summer and winter for the resulting sun spaces. Sadly, cost limitations prevented this being developed further.

In the event, refurbishment was put on hold while designs were prepared for a new-build scheme on a vacant site at the lower (east) end of the terrace. The site, on the corner of Cromartie Road and Hornsey Rise, provided an opportunity to build 20 one- and two-bedroom flats to enhanced low energy standards. The building turns the corner and steps down from five to three storeys to enclose a protected south-facing communal garden. All the living spaces and main bedrooms face south, many with generous balconies, while the kitchens and bathrooms are located on the building's north side.

Construction was in loadbearing masonry with 100mm fully filled cavities and double-glazed windows. The resulting increased investment in the building

Below: ground and typical second floor plans, illustrating the response to both the corner and the site's solar orientation, while the south-facing elevation *(right)* shows large double-glazed windows and a generous balcony for each flat.

Second Floor Plan

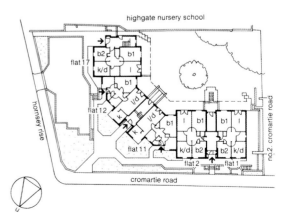

The balconies and private areas overlooking the communal garden are much loved by the residents and nearly all have been generously planted.

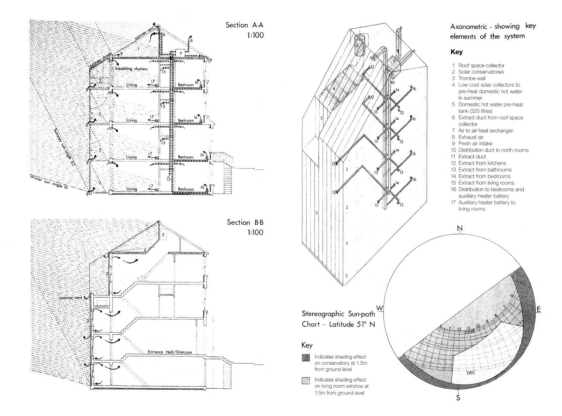

Section A-A
1:100

Section B-B
1:100

Axonometric - showing key elements of the system

Key

1 Roof space collector
2 Solar conservatories
3 Trombe wall
4 Low cost solar collectors to pre-heat domestic hot water in summer
5 Domestic hot water pre-heat tank (320 litres)
6 Extract duct from roof space collector
7 Air to air heat exchanger
8 Exhaust air
9 Fresh air intake
10 Distribution duct to north rooms
11 Extract duct
12 Extract from kitchens
13 Extract from bathrooms
14 Extract from bedrooms
15 Extract from living rooms
16 Distribution to bedrooms and auxiliary heater battery
17 Auxiliary heater battery to living rooms

Stereographic Sun-path Chart - Latitude 51° N

Key

Indicates shading effect on conservatory at 1.5m from ground level

Indicates shading effect on living room window at 1.5m from ground level

The unbuilt EC Passive Solar competition entry showing the addition of a glazed skin to the south facade of the existing terrace.

fabric was offset, however, by a smaller, cheaper central heating system in each flat, properly sized for the small heat loads. On the advice of British Gas, the Gledhill Cormorant system was selected as its small boiler, serving a 120-litre thermal store, was compact and had a fast response time and low running costs. Indeed, the cost for space and water heating was estimated to be 48 per cent of that for equivalent flats built to 1985 Building Regulations standards.

The scheme represented a further development of the principles established at Giffard Park and received an RIBA Energy Efficiency Award in 1988. Following this, ECD commenced refurbishment of the Victorian houses in Cromartie Road, and then completed the development with a second new-build scheme of 12 flats at the upper (west) end of the terrace. This adopted a different approach architecturally, with the two new-build schemes acting as 'bookends' to the imposing Victorian terrace. Altogether, the project took 10 years to complete, but the Co-operative has flourished and the residents, many of them the original inhabitants, remain very happy with their accommodation.

Drawing of the north-facing street elevation showing the new-build additions that act as 'bookends' at either end of the Victorian terrace.

An overall view of the communal south-facing garden, a quiet, green haven where residents can relax.

The final new-build phase at the western end of the Victorian terrace, with its curved metal roof and an early example of a communal roof garden.

Right: a section through the building with its north-facing saw-tooth rooflights, and *(below)* the east and solid south elevations showing one of the external plant rooms and its duct runs.

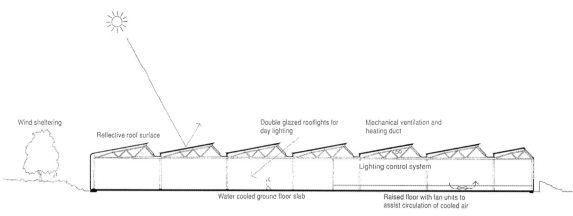

Wind sheltering

Reflective roof surface

Double glazed rooflights for day lighting

Mechanical ventilation and heating duct

Lighting control system

Water cooled ground floor slab

Raised floor with fan units to assist circulation of cooled air

In 1985 Milton Keynes Development Corporation designated 60 hectares in Knowlhill and Shenley Lodge as an 'Energy Park', to showcase the best in low energy design for both residential and commercial sectors. A two stage competition was launched for the design and development of a 'B1' industrial/R&D building on a 0.9 hectare site, with a brief that required the building to perform 40 per cent better than the CIBSE guideline of the time, namely 33.5 W/m^2.

ECD teamed up with developer Bride Hall Group and Ove Arup as engineer, and our proposal was selected as winner on its architectural merit, energy performance and commercial viability. The design provided a flexible, single-storey building of 3653 square metres, with a minimum floor to ceiling height of four metres. The north-facing sawtooth roof profile admitted uniform daylighting across the whole plan area, while minimising solar gain, and the building was designed with a well insulated and well sealed fabric.

Mechanical services were located on the outside of the building envelope, with two plant rooms at opposite ends of the building, supplying fresh air via external ducts to the internal distribution system above ceiling level. The same system heats the building in winter, while

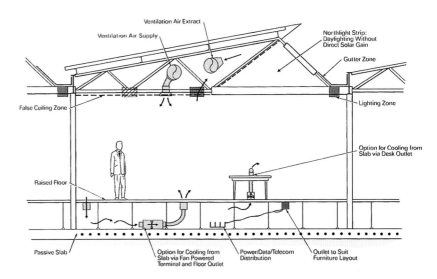

A detail section showing the ground slab cooling and ventilation systems.

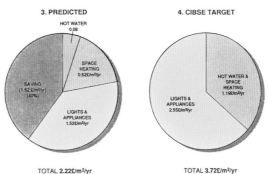

TOTAL 2.22£/m²/yr   TOTAL 3.72£/m²/yr

N.B. 1987 fuel prices: Gas @ 37p/therm
Electricity @ 5.1p/unit

Arup's pie-chart diagrams showing the predicted annual energy costs and savings in relation to the standard CIBSE target of the time.

Detail of one of the external plant rooms, with its glazed facade putting the building's advanced systems on show.

A view of the building from the north-east showing the main entrance into the fully glazed north elevation and the eastern plant room with its external ductwork and freestanding evaporative cooling tower.

A view of the main reception, flooded with daylight from the north-facing rooflights above and the fully glazed north elevation.

the concrete ground floor slab acts as a 'cool store' in summer. A network of polythene pipes was installed in the thickness of the slab and connected to a conventional water-based evaporative cooling tower, which operated on off-peak electricity. This allowed chilled water to pre-cool the structure at night, with small fans located under the raised floor circulating cooled air through the work-space during the day.

An independent assessment of the energy efficiency of the design confirmed a CIBSE Building Energy Demand of 19.9 W/m^2 — 41 per cent better than the set CIBSE guidelines. Low energy design strategies were also employed in a number of other commercial developments in Milton Keynes, including Tarrant House and Noble House in Linford Wood, with both buildings achieving a BREEAM Excellent rating.

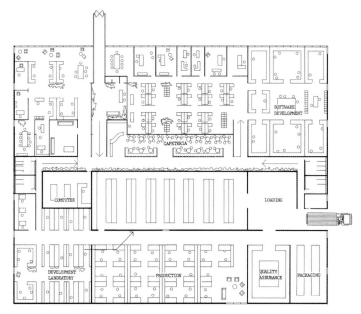

The final floor plan of the building (to a fit-out by Pringle Brandon), with its clear demarcation between office, research and production areas.

An interior view of the main office space along the northern side of the building, with its raised floor in place.

Shenley Lodge Milton Keynes Residential New Build 1991

Moulsham Street Chelmsford Offices and Retail New Build 1992

Linford Wood Milton Keynes Offices New Build 1992

Boxfield Farm Stevenage Residential New Build 1992

Wrythe Lane Sutton Residential New Build 1993

Barkantine Estate Tower Hamlets Residential Refurbishment 1993

Barleymow Estate Limehouse Residential Refurbishment 1993

IGA Stuttgart Residential New Build 1993

Hazelwood and Adair Towers Kensington Residential Refurbishment 1994

Wornington Green Estate Kensington Residential Refurbishment 1995

Hurst Street Limehouse Residential Refurbishment 1995

Meath House Lambeth Residential Refurbishment 1995

Linacre College Oxford University Residential New Build 1995

Queen's Building Anglia Ruskin University Educational New Build 1995

Whitley Wood Reading Residential New Build 1996

Goldington Street Estate King's Cross Residential Refurbishment 1996

Templeton College Oxford University Lecture Theatre New Build 1997

Team Pictures Mile End Film Editing Suite Refurbishment 1998

Boots Library Nottingham Trent University Library New Build 1998

Rolls Crescent Manchester Residential New Build 1998

Scottish & Newcastle Greenford Warehouse and offices New Build 1998

Rotheley House Hackney Residential Refurbishment 1998

York Road Sutton Residential New Build 1998

Hutchesontown Glasgow Residential Refurbishment 1998

Sawyers Building Anglia Ruskin University Faculty Building New Build 1999

Sancroft Road Harrow Residential Care Centre New Build 1999

Wetlands Conservation Centre Slimbridge New Build 1999

International Building Royal Holloway Faculty Building New Build 1999

1990–2000

2 The Green 1990s

The 1990s were a highly creative time for ECD and, as the UK economy moved out of recession, it became increasingly prolific too. A lot of positive groundwork had been completed during the previous decade. We had learned about the issues, but in some ways it had been a lonely time, with much of the research and development work being undertaken by small groups and individuals working in relative isolation.

The 1990s was the decade when ideas and people began to connect to form a network; it began to feel that a 'sustainable design' community was emerging. We got into the habit of attending research conferences, particularly in Europe, and started to exchange ideas and information with like-minded professionals in places such as Denmark and the Netherlands. Important contacts were made, and out of those emerged some enduring friendships.

We marked the start of the decade with a campaigning exhibition, *Energy Conscious Design into the 1990s*, which was opened at Smiths Gallery in Covent Garden in January 1990 by Jonathon Porritt. The exhibition focused on emerging concerns over global warming, including the greenhouse effect and, in particular, the problem of CO_2 emissions. The exhibition also addressed the damage to the ozone layer caused by CFC gases, the effects of deforestation and acid rain and, most importantly, the part played by buildings in creating these problems and in providing mitigating solutions.

We featured a number of ECD's low energy projects, some completed, some at the design stage, but all offering tried and tested, cost-effective solutions. We highlighted the fact that energy conscious design can halve the quantity of CO_2 put into the atmosphere and asked the question: "Why on earth are these standards not universal now?" We also proposed an environmental mandate for the building industry and called for a new 'Green Label' to reward good environmental practice.

The exhibition was our contribution to the increasingly loud clamour being made by small groups like us, which helped to promote environmental awareness in the early 1990s. This surge in public interest was, in turn, fuelled by the accelerating engagement in some sectors of the media with issues of sustainability, in particular by the campaigning journalism of environmental writers such as David Nicholson-Lord.

When the exhibition closed we wrote to the Department of Environment, setting out our thoughts on the subject in more detail. We were promptly put in touch with the Building Research Establishment (BRE), which was then charged with the task of producing an environmental assessment method for new non-residential buildings, initially offices. This led to our working with the BRE and a key sponsor, Stanhope, to produce BREEAM, the Building Research Establishment Environmental Assessment Method. Now established as the industry standard, this has since been extended by the

ECD 1999, the catalogue for the exhibition ECD held to mark the beginning of the 1990s.

The first BREEAM logo – ECD was closely involved in the development of the assessment methodology.

The 'Green' team – from left to right, the ECD partners David Turrent, John Doggart, Richard Ferraro and David Billingham, photographed for an *Architects' Journal* article in June 1993.

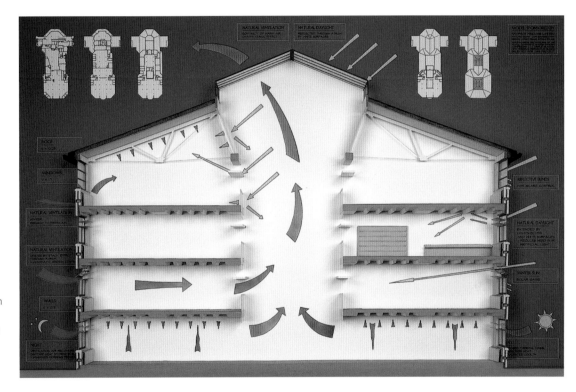

A three-dimensional diagram prepared to explain the key energy conserving principles built into the design of the Queen's Building for Anglia Ruskin University.

BRE, again with ECD's assistance, to cover numerous different building types.

We were particularly interested at this time in extending our low energy approach to a diverse range of building types. We knew that the knowledge we had developed while working mainly on housing projects in the 1980s was inherently transferable. We had been thinking, for instance, about what a 'green' office building might be like and had worked up several speculative designs. In 1993 we were fortunate to be in the right place at the right time when we met Tim Matthews of Anglia Ruskin University, which was then relocating to a new site near Chelmsford. He needed a new campus building and was enthusiastic about our low energy ideas, and that chance encounter led to our first commission in the higher education sector.

Our initial move was to organise an intensive workshop with the client and our collaborators on the project, including the engineer Chris Twinn of Arup. Between us, in the space of just five days (it all happened very quickly), we thrashed out a brief,

Linacre College, Oxford – an internal view of the entrance and main staircase, based like all the floor layouts on the use of organic forms.

The students' cafeteria at the International Building, with its use of soft rounded forms to enhance a sense of calm relaxation.

A diagrammatic section of the Templeton College lecture theatre, showing the under-floor ground source cooling and ventilation system.

Ventilation of stale air from the lecture theatre is much enhanced by the all-glass, 'solar chimney' air vents.

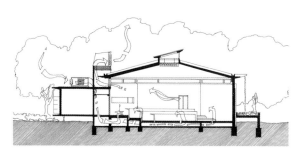

developed design concepts and tested thermal models for what became the Queen's Building, one of the first of a new generation of Learning Resource Centres. This was closely followed by a postgraduate residential building in Oxford for Linacre College, which won 'Green Building of the Year' in 1996, one better than the Queen's Building, which was runner-up. Also in Oxford, we designed a new lecture theatre for Templeton College, using ground source cooling and roof-mounted air vents.

Other university projects followed, including the International Building in Egham for Royal Holloway, part of the University of London, which won an RIBA Regional Architecture Award; the naturally ventilated Sawyers Building, also at Anglia Ruskin University; and the Boots Library building for Nottingham Trent University. This occupied the entire footprint of a triangular city-centre site and was planned around a central 'teardrop'-shaped atrium – a device which enhances the legibility of such a large and complex building type.

The south elevation of the
Sawyers Building at Anglia
Ruskin University, with its
triple-glazed windows and
purpose-designed sunshades.

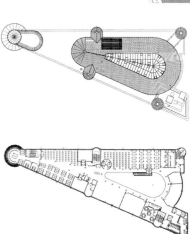

Right: the triangular shaped site plan and urban context of the Boots Library in Nottingham, with *(below)* the floor plans illustrating the flexible open-plan spaces around the central atrium.

Boots Library — the internal teardrop-shaped atrium provides daylight deep into the heart of the building.

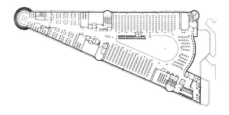

A view of one of the secure new semi-private entrance courtyards to the refurbished flats of the Barleymow Estate, Limehouse.

The Boots Library has 9000 square metres of accommodation planned on five levels, including a 300-seat lecture theatre in the basement. The highly insulated building is heated and cooled using the TermoDeck system, which circulates fresh air through the floor structure to achieve stable internal temperatures and reduced energy consumption. As it turned out, our 1990 exhibition proved to be a marker in the development of the UK's thinking about the heating and cooling of buildings, and coincided with the shift towards more integrated design of building fabric and engineering services.

During the recession of the early 1990s, ECD survived by concentrating on large public sector regeneration projects, including the low energy refurbishment of residential tower blocks and

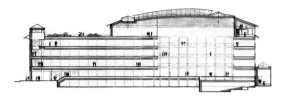

A section through the five-storey Boots Library, which utilises the TermoDeck heating and cooling system.

numerous run-down 1960s council estates. In Limehouse, Tower Hamlets, for example, we carried out extensive repairs and improvements to the Barley-mow and Barkantine Estates. Resident consultation was — and remains — a central aspect of this work, creating stronger communities that retain a sense of 'ownership' over the solutions created. We regard this as an important part of the social aspect of

The Barkantine Estate before (above) and after (top) refurbishment. New double-glazed windows and an application of insulated render reduced CO_2 emissions by 50 per cent.

ECD undertook the comprehensive refurbishment of a number of residential towers during the 1990s, including Hazelwood Tower *(far left)*, the Hurst Street Estate *(left)* and Meath House *(below)*, an eight-storey block with a curved metal roof.

The north-facing elevation of the IGA' 93 houses in Stuttgart, complete with small windows and steeply sloping zinc roofs.

sustainability, alongside the economic and environmental aspects addressed by ECD's physical low energy solutions.

Since the 1990s, this work has been extended to address wider urban regeneration projects and masterplans. Overall, we have refurbished more than 20,000 older dwellings, including more than 20 tower blocks, such as Hazelwood and Adair towers in north Kensington and Meath House in Lambeth. Through this work the useful life of buildings has been extended, with thousands of tonnes of CO_2

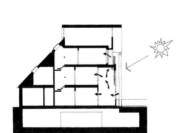

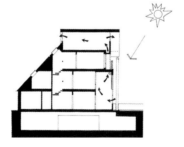

Sections through the IGA '93 houses showing summer and winter ventilation modes.

saved annually. Fuel poverty has also been alleviated, the security of residents improved, and the visual quality of the built environment enhanced.

In 1991 we won an international competition for three 'eco' houses, to be built as part of an exhibition within the 1993 International Garden Festival in Stuttgart — to date our only built scheme outside the UK. The houses were of solid concrete

The south elevation of the
IGA '93 houses in Stuttgart,
each with its own double-
height conservatory.

The site plan of the Boxfield Farm estate, with its mixture of orthogonal and wedge-shaped house plans.

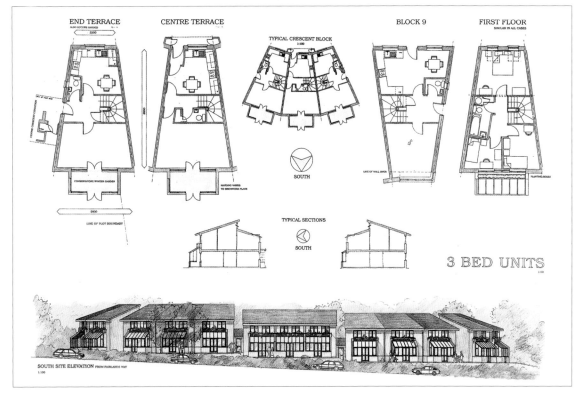

END TERRACE ALSO OCCURS HANDED 3000

CENTRE TERRACE

TYPICAL CRESCENT BLOCK 1:100

BLOCK 9

FIRST FLOOR SIMILAR IN ALL CASES

SOUTH

CONSERVATORY/WINTER GARDEN

5800 LINE OF PLOT BOUNDARY

HANDING VARIES TO BRICKWORK FLOOR

SOUTH

LINE OF WALL OVER

PLANTING BOXES

TYPICAL SECTIONS

SOUTH

3 BED UNITS 1:50

SOUTH SITE ELEVATION FROM FAIRLANDS WAY 1:100

Boxfield Farm — the floor plans of the various wedge-shaped houses, including those with south-facing conservatories.

A view of Boxfield Farm from the east, looking into the heart of the scheme and showing the south-facing clerestory windows.

Final design proposal for the partially sunk, earth-covered Mile End Park Sports Centre, sadly unbuilt.

construction, with external insulation and large sun spaces integrated into each unit. Meanwhile, we continued designing low energy housing schemes for housing associations in the UK. At Boxfield Farm in Stevenage, we developed a wedge-shaped house plan, facing south with a conservatory extension to the living room. This was one of the first schemes to be awarded a BREEAM Environmental Assessment Rating, a forerunner of 'EcoHomes'. We also designed a 50-bed care home in Sancroft Road,

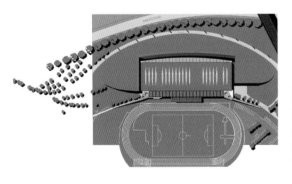

Site plan of the Mile End Park Sports Centre, showing the relationship to the existing athletics track and the public circulation route through the 'winter garden'.

Harrow, using passive solar principles and well insulated timber frame construction.

In 1996 we participated in a planning weekend organised by Tower Hamlets Council and the Environment Trust, to generate ideas for the future of Mile End Park. Among many positive outcomes, including the Piers Gough designed 'green bridge' crossing Mile End Road, was a commission for ECD and Proctor and Matthews Architects to design a new sports building in the park. The idea, which was developed to planning stage, was for a partially

Sancroft Road, Harrow – a 50-bed care home built in a well insulated timber frame construction around a south-facing courtyard

The distinctive rendered towers overlooking the main street intersections at Rolls Crescent, Hulme.

Rotheley House, Hackney — a refurbished 1960s concrete-frame building with flats located above a ground floor housing office.

An early concept sketch for
the observation tower of
the Wetlands Conservation
Centre at Slimbridge.

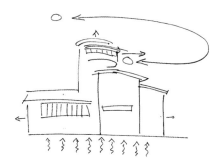

sunk, earth-covered building enclosing 'wet' and 'dry' facilities, with a dramatic glazed street connecting the building to playing fields in the park and providing viewing facilities for spectators. Sadly this exciting building was never built.

Rotheley House in Hackney was completed in 1998. This was a 1960s building that we stripped back to the concrete frame and refurbished to provide 13 new flats for people with learning disabilities. The extended ground floor provides office accommodation for Hackney's neighbourhood Housing Office. Externally the building was clad in white insulated render and cedar cladding to give it a clean contemporary appearance. New-build housing schemes were also being completed in York Road, Sutton, and at Hulme in Manchester, with the latter hailed as an exemplar of good urban design and featured as a case study in the CABE publication, *By Design – Better Places to Live.*

Towards the end of the decade, lottery-funded Millennium projects offered opportunities and we were successful in winning two high profile projects, a new museum in Banbury (completed in 2002) and the Wetlands Conservation Centre at Slimbridge in Gloucestershire, headquarters of the Wildfowl and Wetlands Trust. The site at Slimbridge offered exciting possibilities: a flat uninterrupted landscape with views across the Severn Estuary and a group of buildings urgently in need of remodelling. Both projects were demanding one-off pieces of architecture, incorporating exemplary standards of

Above and right: the highly insulated care home at York Road, Sutton, with its copper roof and brick and timber cladding.

sustainability within modest budgets. They have also proved equally successful, with visitor numbers to both far exceeding expectations.

1995 saw a restructuring of the practice into two separate companies: ECD Architects Ltd and ECD Energy and Environment Ltd. David Turrent and Richard Ferraro expanded the architectural practice, with David Billingham's help as a director until he moved on in 1997. John Doggart led the energy team with support from associates Miles

Design proposal for the Greenwich Millennium Village competition, prepared in association with Countryside Properties.

The final report of the EC Energy Comfort 2000 project, a study of nine exemplar European projects, including ECD's Queen's Building at Anglia Ruskin University.

Attenborough and Simon Burton. During the 1990s the energy team undertook numerous BREEAM assessments for commercial and public sector clients, as well as participating in the production of new versions for retail and industrial buildings.

The European Commission remained a key client, commissioning dissemination projects such as 'THERMIE' and 'Energy Comfort 2000', for which ECD was appointed co-ordinator of European projects – leading us to set up an office in Brussels (run by Simon Burton) in 1994. Energy Comfort 2000 showcased nine new office and university buildings in the Netherlands, France, Germany, Greece, Spain and Portugal, while the UK was represented by ECD's own Queen's Building at Anglia Ruskin University. The buildings all had the common aim of reducing the need for traditional air conditioning, while providing healthier and more environmentally friendly places to work.

The 1990s was characterised by a number of exemplar low energy projects, in the main led by public sector clients, while the private sec-tor remained wedded to minimum regulatory standards. Sustainability started becoming common currency in the latter half of the decade, defined by a checklist of features including energy, water, waste, transport and biodiversity. Although energy and CO_2 emissions were perceived as the key issues for building designers, the wider issues gained in importance and a holistic approach emerged as the new mantra. This included the 'triple bottom line' benefits of a truly sustainable approach – social, economic and environmental.

One of our main objectives was to ensure that sustainability and high quality design were not mutually exclusive, but ideally went hand in hand. Winning design awards and competitions has been at least as important to us as achieving BREEAM 'Excellent' ratings. One interesting competition entry around this time – designed with Max Fordham LLP and featured in the 1996 Venice Biennale – was for a Science and Engineering Library (SELLIC) at the University of London, incorporating a long south-facing winter garden.

The shortlisted competition entry for the naturally ventilated SELLIC library, exhibited at the 1996 Venice Biennale.

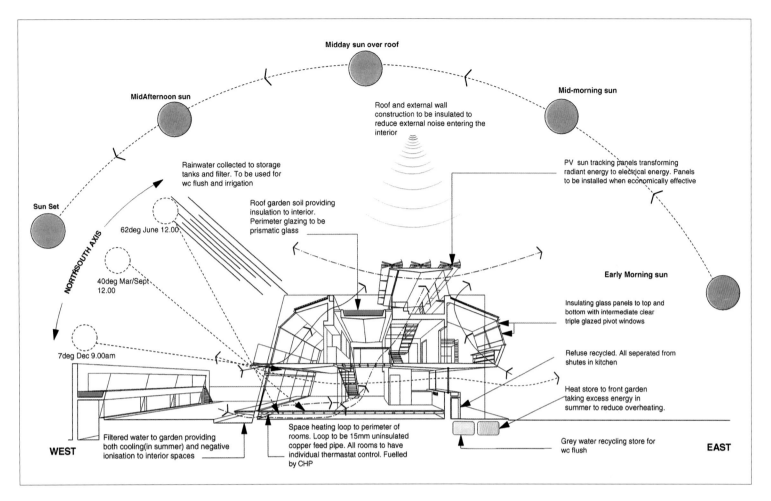

Midday sun over roof

MidAfternoon sun

Mid-morning sun

Roof and external wall construction to be insulated to reduce external noise entering the interior

Sun Set

Rainwater collected to storage tanks and filter. To be used for wc flush and irrigation

PV sun tracking panels transforming radiant energy to electrical energy. Panels to be installed when economically effective

NORTH&SOUTH AXIS

62deg June 12.00

Roof garden soil providing insulation to interior. Perimeter glazing to be prismatic glass

Early Morning sun

40deg Mar/Sept 12.00

Insulating glass panels to top and bottom with intermediate clear triple glazed pivot windows

7deg Dec 9.00am

Refuse recycled. All seperated from shutes in kitchen

Heat store to front garden taking excess energy in summer to reduce overheating.

WEST

Filtered water to garden providing both cooling(in summer) and negative ionisation to interior spaces

Space heating loop to perimeter of rooms. Loop to be 15mm uninsulated copper feed pipe. All rooms to have individual thermastat control. Fuelled by CHP

Grey water recycling store for wc flush

EAST

A diagrammatic section illustrating the passive solar and environmental strategies for ECD's competition-winning zero CO_2 housing at Newark.

By the end of the 1990s, Ecohomes had become the benchmark for assessment of new social housing, and BREEAM had established itself as the industry wide standard for non-domestic buildings. Also, attention and interest began to shift from individual, exemplar low energy buildings towards the construction of larger sustainable communities. John Prescott, the Deputy Prime Minister, launched the Millennium Villages competition, including a substantial new 'village' to be constructed on the derelict and much contaminated Greenwich Peninsula in east London.

As attempted in the Energy Park project at Milton Keynes in the late 1980s (a victim of the early '90s recession), the Millennium Village project set specific standards for energy and water consumption, as well as limits on waste generation during construction. Our entry for Greenwich — carried out in association with EDAW, PRP, Allies and Morrison and John Pardey — was not successful. In 1999, however, ECD won the BRE-sponsored 'Zero CO_2' design competition for 67 houses and flats on a site adjacent to the River Trent in Newark, with a high quality architectural solution fuelled by a biomass CHP (combined heat and power) plant.

After five years trading as a separate company, ECD Energy and Environment Ltd was acquired by Faber Maunsell in 2000 and now forms an important part of the worldwide AECOM Group. ECD and AECOM continue to collaborate and, in 2010, are joint partners with United House in the '80/80 Partnership', a multi-disciplinary team with the aim of reducing CO_2 emissions by 80 per cent in 80 per cent of the existing housing stock by 2050.

The Barleymow Estate

Tower Hamlets, London 1993

Below: resident consultation
in action at the Barleymow
Estate

Entrance to the tower block
before and after refurbishment, illustrating the overall
visual enhancement and the
much improved security,
lighting and landscaping.

The Barleymow Estate in Limehouse consisted of three 14-storey tower blocks, each containing 56 flats, surrounded by a further 72 flats accommodated in three-storey blocks. They were built in 1968 using Taylor Woodrow's Anglian precast-concrete system – similar in concept to Ronan Point, which infamously collapsed as a result of a minor gas explosion. One of the three towers needed to be demolished to make way for the 'Limehouse Link' road to the Isle

of Dogs but, as compensation, funding was allocated to refurbish the remainder of the estate.

In 1990 ECD was appointed by Tower Hamlets Council to work on a feasibility study with the Residents Association. The tenants were in broad agreement about their problems, which they listed as expensive heating, poor comfort, condensation and mould, draughts, noise, security, poor lighting and insufficient parking. In addition to the essential structural strengthening of the towers, we therefore proposed insulated overcladding to improve the thermal performance of the building fabric. A Sto acrylic render system was specified with 100mm thermal insulation, giving a U value of 0.26 W/m^2.K. The advantage of this approach was that it eliminated leaks and cold bridging and enabled use to be made of the thermal mass of the structure.

Double glazed windows had already been installed as part of an earlier contract. Heating was provided by electric off-peak storage heaters and hot water by Economy 7. Trickle ventilation had to be retrofitted to the windows, to minimise the condensation risk. Each tower was connected to a centralised 'concierge' office, installed with estate-wide CCTV monitors, while external security was improved with better lighting and a restructuring of the public and semi-public areas, combined with extensive landscaping.

As a result, both the appearance and safety of the estate were transformed. The process of consultation brought the community closer together and tenants continue to report that they are proud to live on the estate.

The Barleymow tower after refurbishment with Sto's insulated overcladding.

The newly refurbished Barleymow Estate in the context of Canary Wharf and the Isle of Dogs.

Linacre College

Oxford   1994

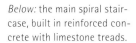
The new extension adopted a traditional design to match the style of the existing building.

Below: the main spiral staircase, built in reinforced concrete with limestone treads.

Interior of one of the distinctive study bedrooms, with the natural timber fittings and finishes reinforcing the organic plan form.

When the opportunity arose to build new student accommodation at the residential postgraduate Linacre College, the brief from principal Sir Bryan Cartledge (who had been our ambassador in Moscow at the time of the Chernobyl disaster) could not have been simpler: "I want the greenest building in the UK."

Appointed in 1991, ECD inherited an external design that matched the style of the existing college building – a turn of the century red brick building with Dutch

gables. We chose to focus, therefore, on the design of the interior spaces – 23 study bedrooms together with ancillary study and storage areas. Perhaps as a reaction to the formal exterior, we based our solution on non-rectilinear planning, the more informal, organic layout giving each of the rooms its own identity.

In order to maximise development potential, we also introduced a full basement housing a fitness and recreation area and a music practice room. The student accommodation itself is arranged on four levels with access provided by a dramatic spiral staircase finished with limestone treads. Study rooms are located in the roof space.

In line with passive design principles, all living spaces face south with service areas to the north, and an embodied energy audit was undertaken during the design phase. The main construction was loadbearing masonry with 125mm filled cavities, while the roof space was filled with 150mm blown Warmcel insulation. Heating was provided by a condensing gas boiler and ventilation by passive stack effect. Low energy lighting was installed throughout and a grey water recycling system was installed to supply the lavatory cisterns.

Estimated energy needs showed a 35 per cent reduction in gas consumption compared to 1990 Building Regulations, and a 25 per cent reduction in electricity, while CO_2 emissions were estimated to be 39kg/m^2/yr, which the College offset by spending £10,000 to adopt 40 acres of threatened eucalyptus forest in Tasmania. The building was completed in 1994 and achieved a BREEAM 'Excellent' rating, going on to win the Green Building of the Year Award in 1996.

Views of the entrance to the
building and the limestone
spiral staircase.

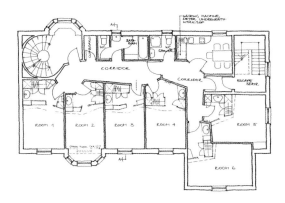

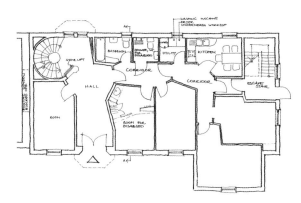

Plans of the main entrance
level and a typical student
floor, the non-orthogonal
geometry giving individu-
ality to each study bedroom.

A three-dimensional diagram
showing the 'green' features
of the project, which won
'Green Building of the Year'
in 1996.

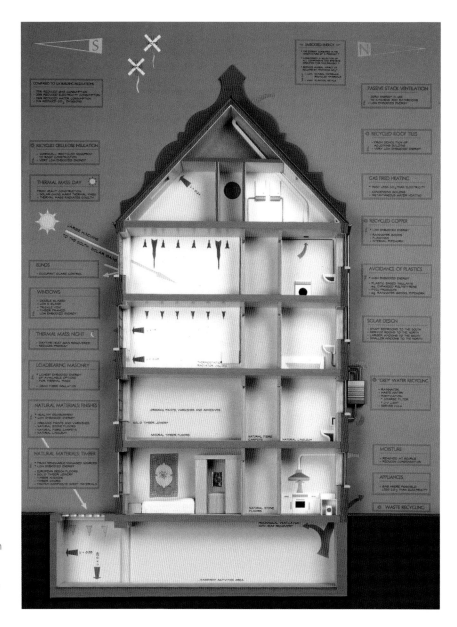

Queen's Building

Anglia Ruskin University, Chelmsford   1995

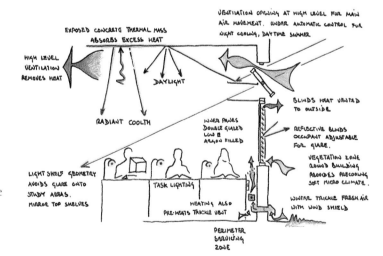

A sketch section showing the daylighting and natural stack effect ventilation strategies for the building as a whole.

A more detailed sketch of the environmental strategies in the perimeter study areas.

A site plan of Queen's Building, set at right angles to the river and indicating the site of the later Sawyers Building.

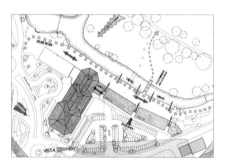

In the early 1990s Anglia Polytechnic University (now Anglia Ruskin University) decided to relocate their campus from Chelmsford city centre to the new River-mead campus next to the River Chelmer, the centrepiece of which was to be a state-of-the-art, low energy Learning Resource Centre. ECD and Arup were appointed to prepare design proposals.

The first step was a week-long briefing and design workshop, involving client user groups and European experts in low energy design strategies. From this a design concept emerged for a 6100 square-metre, deep plan building on three and four levels, with two central atria providing daylighting and stack effect ventilation. The proportions of the atria spaces were modelled under an artificial sky, while dynamic thermal modelling of the whole building allowed internal temperatures and comfort conditions to be predicted with a high degree of accuracy.

The west elevation and a corresponding long section through the north and south atria.

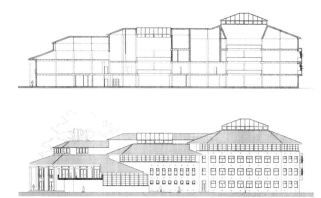

Internal view of the south atrium at night showing the open floor plans with the library stacks around the atrium edge.

Thermal mass plays an important part in the environmental strategy, as do the triple-glazed windows with inter-pane blinds that minimise solar gain but maximise good daylighting. The objective was to achieve an annual energy consumption 45 per cent lower than for a comparable air-conditioned building — equivalent to 90 kWh/m²/yr. Additional funding for extra capital costs and performance monitoring was obtained through the EU 'THERMIE' programme.

The project timescale was fast. The briefing workshop took place in March 2003, site construction commenced in July and the building was completed by the following summer. A PROBE study carried out two years later measured the actual energy consumption and user satisfaction. Generally, the building has performed well, with night cooling of the structure proving particularly effective in stabilising internal temperatures.

Annual energy consumption was measured at 132 kWh/m²/yr, as energy use for lighting was higher than anticipated. Overall daylight distribution could also have been improved in some areas. One negative aspect of user feedback concerned noise in the atrium, but this was addressed by better space management. The University is very pleased with the building.

Opposite: an upper floor overlooking the atrium with its light screens and horizontal daylight diffusers.

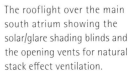
The rooflight over the main south atrium showing the solar/glare shading blinds and the opening vents for natural stack effect ventilation.

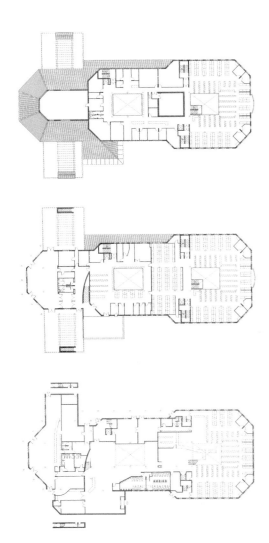
The ground, first and second floors showing the distribution of study spaces around the perimeter of the building.

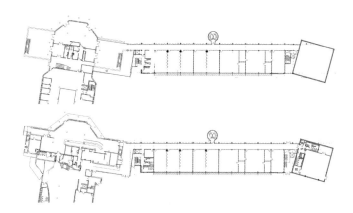

The ground and typical upper floor plan showing the link to the adjacent Queen's Building and the new building's single aspect teaching spaces.

The south elevation with its extensive use of accurately designed *brises-soleil* to precisely shade the south-facing glazing.

Sawyers Building

Anglia Ruskin University, Chelmsford   1999

The masterplan for the development of the new Rivermead campus at Anglia Ruskin University in Chelmsford always envisaged extensions to the northern end of the Queen's Building. In 1996 ECD was given the opportunity of designing a new Faculty of Education on a long thin strip of land to the north-east of the Queen's Building, overlooking the River Chelmer and the water meadows to the north. The brief was for a 5000 square-metre building incorporating a wide range of flexible teaching spaces, laboratories, a music suite, offices and a multipurpose sports hall, all designed to

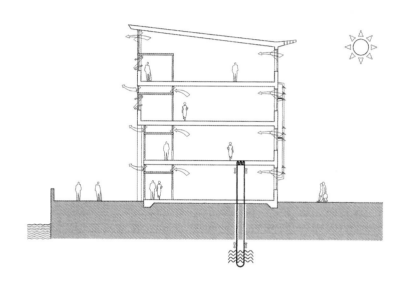

A detail view of the *brises-soleil* that run the length of the south elevation.

low energy 'green' standards that are economic to run and maintain.

Our approach was to plan the accommodation on four floors, utilising the full length of the site while limiting the depth of the building to just 13 metres, enabling good daylighting and cross-ventilation on all floors. Circulation is

principally on the north side of the building with dropped ceilings to allow a ventilation route to the external wall, while the construction was steel frame and precast concrete floors with exposed soffits to utilise the thermal mass. The building management system (BMS) opens and closes high level windows automatically at night to 'pre-cool' the structure in summer.

The building has a distinctive appearance that expresses the simple, passive approach to achieving a low energy solution, and is considered an exemplar for non-domestic sustainable architecture. It was completed in 1999 and obtained a BREEAM 'Excellent' rating.

A section through Sawyers Building showing the cross-ventilation strategy, and a borehole heat exchanger not included in the final design.

Rolls Crescent

Hulme, Manchester 1998

Site plan showing the three
urban blocks, each with
traditional street frontages
and small private gardens
overlooking a secure inner
courtyard.

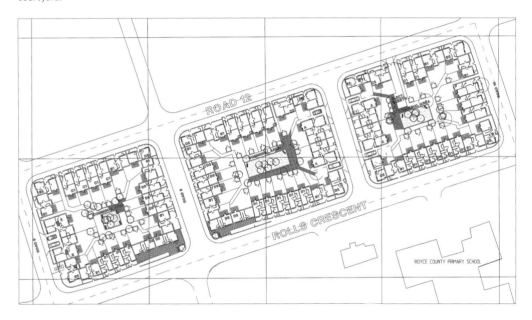

Typical long and short elevations of the central block.

Completed in 1968, the infamous Rolls
Crescent housing blocks were demolished
in 1994 to make way for a new masterplan. Accompanied by an Urban Design
Code, developed by MBLC Architects and
Urbanists and initiated by the local community, this was based on a traditional
street pattern. ECD participated in the
resident consultation process and submitted schemes for several competitions
before being awarded a site on the
southern edge of the masterplan by the
North British Housing Association — now
called Places for People.

The brief called for 67 family homes,
provided in three urban blocks with a
mix of single-, two- and three-storey
terraced houses, laid out to reflect the
hierarchy of the street pattern. With the
exception of wheelchair dwellings, all
front doors face on to the street — where
cars are also parked — with a small semi-
private area separating them from the

An exploded view of one
of the three-storey corner
houses, with its top floor
roof garden overlooking the
inner courtyard.

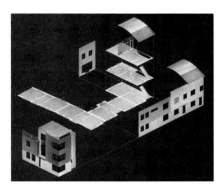

A view over one of the inner courtyards with its mixture of private and communal gardens as well as a view of the city beyond.

A typical street elevation with its rendered facade, projecting bay windows and on-street parking.

public realm. Corner windows provide natural surveillance of the streets, while key intersections are marked by a distinctive three-storey 'tower' house. To the rear, all houses have small private gardens that overlook secure communal areas within the inner courtyards.

Construction is in loadbearing brickwork with 100mm filled cavities, while the 'warm', standing seam curved roofs are insulated with 150mm mineral wool and the flat roofs and terraces with cork. Ventilation is achieved using the passive 'whole house' system, where moist air is extracted from kitchens and bathrooms by stack effect. Air inlet vents were fitted in external walls – automatically opening and closing according to internal humidity levels.

Richard Strittmatter, manager of the Hulme Partnership from 1991 to 1996, probably best summed up the success of the scheme when he commented, "the Hulme City Challenge would probably be described as one of the first examples of new urbanism in the UK. Rolls Crescent, with its distinctive curved silver roofs and colourful rendered walls and roof gardens has become known locally as 'Club Med'. It is unashamedly contemporary and has sustainability credentials far in excess of the statutory requirements that applied at the time".

An overview of all three blocks, with the corner windows of the distinctive 'tower' houses at each end of a block offering maximum natural surveillance of the public realm.

Construction details for one of the three-storey mid-terrace houses, each with its own roof garden and curved metal roof.

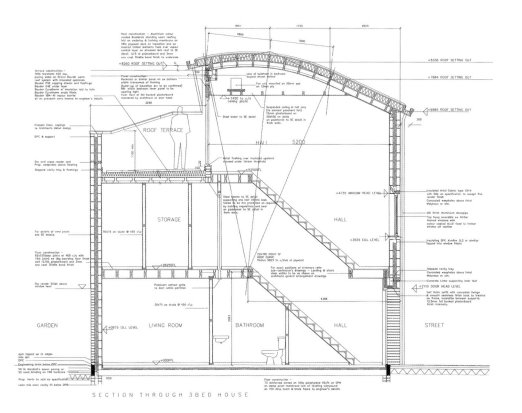

SECTION THROUGH 3 BED HOUSE

An early concept sketch illustrating the building's orientation and ventilation strategy.

The main south elevation, with the windows protected from the sun by a system of sliding louvre shutters.

International Building

Royal Holloway, University of London   1999

The Royal Holloway campus in Egham is dominated by the Grade 1 Listed Founder's Building but has, over the years, accumulated a number of other distinctive buildings. In 1996, the College held a competitive interview process to select an architect to design a new academic building, with a brief to amalgamate all the language departments (previously housed in temporary buildings) into a single Faculty building of around 4000 square metres. ECD was successful with a U-shaped proposal that turns its back on the busy A30 (which runs along the northern boundary) to form a new south-facing external space between it and the Students' Union building opposite.

Accommodation consists mainly of cellular offices spread over three floors, together with seminar rooms, language laboratories and a café. The sloping site allowed the main double-height entrance to be positioned at first floor level, thereby reducing the bulk of the building.

The client was keen to adopt a 'green' approach, so emphasis was placed on good daylighting, natural ventilation and exposed thermal mass. Motorised vents are located at the ends of the hollow-core concrete floor slabs to enable night cooling of the structure, while manually controlled external shutters can be used to minimise solar gain and glare. In areas with higher cooling loads, fresh air is drawn through a labyrinth of low brick walls below the ground floor slab.

The building is clad in untreated western red cedar over a red brick base, in response to the Founder's Hall, while the monopitch roof has a standing-seam aluminium finish, dished inwards from the road to emphasise the building's domestic scale. Well liked by staff and students alike, the building won an RIBA Architecture Award in 1999.

The double-height entrance and reception area at the first-floor level.

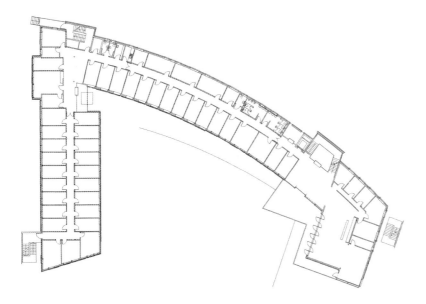

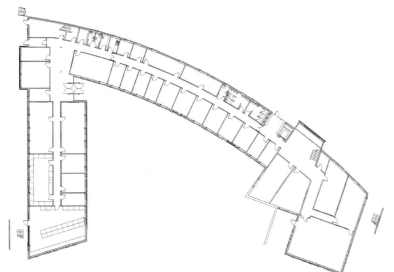

Opposite: a detail view of the building from the south-east, with the upper two levels clad in cedar over a ground floor base of red brick.

The main entrance terrace at first floor level.

The first floor plan *(top)* with the main entrance to the right. Together with the ground *(above)* and second floors, the interior is given over entirely to small cellular offices, seminar rooms and larger teaching laboratories.

The building stands well above the road, and is approached via a long staircase leading up to the main entrance on the first floor.

1990–2000

Wetlands Conservation Centre

Slimbridge, Gloucestershire 1999

An early concept sketch showing the building surrounded by water.

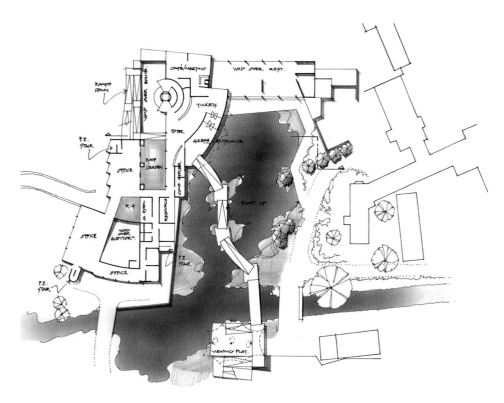

The first floor plan showing the new entrance sequence for visitors, via a ramped boardwalk over a new expanse of water in front of the building, leading to the first floor entrance.

In 1995 we received a fax from the Wildfowl and Wetlands Trust asking if we would be interested in preparing a feasibility study for the redevelopment of their HQ at Slimbridge. We teamed up with Landscape Design Associates (LDA) and submitted a formal 'expression of interest', together with some preliminary design ideas.

Little had changed since Sir Peter Scott had established his bird sanctuary and nature centre there in the 1950s and, despite its beautiful setting, our initial impressions of the previous facilities were somewhat underwhelming. LDA proposed the creation of a new lake in front of an expanded reception building, to allow visitors an early view of water and birdlife, while we developed ideas for a new 18-metre-high observation tower that was a requirement of the outline brief. This was intended to give the building real presence in the flat landscape, while allowing visitors longer views over the wetlands of the Severn Estuary.

After winning a competitive interview, ECD was appointed to carry out the initial feasibility study, leading to the development of a new site masterplan. This was refined through a series of design workshops held on site with key stakeholders, which formed the basis for a successful application to the Millennium

A sectional elevation presented as part of ECD and LDA's initial submission.

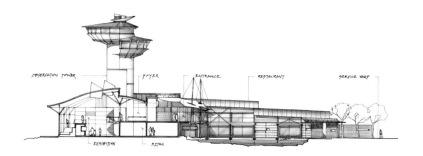

OBSERVATION TOWER   FOYER   ENTRANCE   RESTAURANT   SERVICE YARD

EXHIBITION   RETAIL

View of the completed building with its integration of new and existing/refurbished elements. The organic forms and natural materials were designed to blend in with the wetlands environment.

A gentle ramp offers visitors easy access from the entry hall above to the exhibition areas on the ground floor.

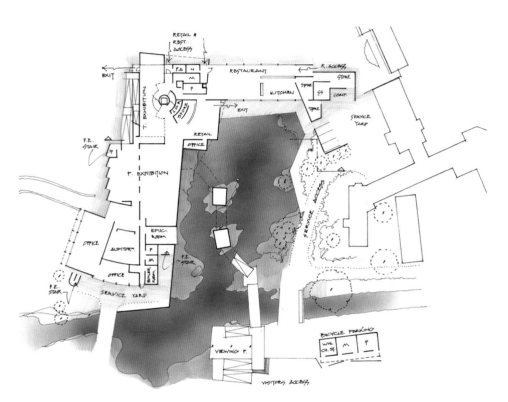

All the main visitor facilities — including exhibition areas, an auditorium, a shop and a café — are located on the ground floor.

Lottery Fund. This allowed us to proceed to a detailed planning application that mixed some refurbishment with extensive new-build facilities. In addition to the new observation tower, the scheme provided new entrance and exhibition areas, a restaurant, a shop, office space and two houses for site staff.

A good deal of time was spent developing the brief with the client, resulting in an architectural solution that resolved all the functional, aesthetic and environmental requirements. The building's use of brick, render and untreated cedar — including the gently curved cedar shingle roofs — all serve to reinforce the horizontal emphasis of the building and its natural setting. Large glazed areas also provide visual connections between inside and outside, so that one is always aware of the presence of nature and the wildlife. The building makes use of good daylighting and the exhibition spaces at the lower level are ventilated by passive stack effect. Rainwater is collected and recycled for use in the lavatories, and all waste water is treated in a reed bed and returned to the water bodies.

At £3.6m the building represented good value for money and was completed in time for the Millennium. The project won a Civic Trust Award in 2001 and now receives over 300,000 visitors a year.

Visitors enter the building via a raised boardwalk over a newly created body of water.

An internal view of the main entrance hall, with the ticket and information desk wrapping round the central drum that supports the observation tower above.

Detail view of the ramp leading down to visitor facilities and access to the wetlands walks on the ground floor.

A view of the timber-clad, shingle roofed building from the Slimbridge wetlands, with the ventilation 'chimneys' over the refurbished exhibition space clearly visible.

Entertainment UK Greenford Warehouse and Offices New Build 2000

Seaton Point London Residential Refurbishment 2000

Mason Moor Southampton Residential New Build 2000

Birchensale Middle School Redditch Extension and Refurbishment 2002

Banbury Museum Oxfordshire Museum New Build 2002

The Royal Ballet School London Dance Studios and Retail New Build 2002

Eider Close London Residential New Build 2003

Roscoe Towers London Residential Refurbishment 2004

36 Beaufort Gardens London Residential Refurbishment 2004

Olive Mount Liverpool Residential New Build 2005

Coopers Road London Residential New Build 2005

Radoon Cornwall Private Residence New Build 2006

Kings Court Cambridge Industrial New Build 2007

Broadclose Farm Cornwall Residential New Build 2006

Cliveden Village Buckinghamshire Residential New Build 2007

Rockmount School Croydon School Extension and Refurbishment 2008

Wolseley Building Centre Leamington Spa Showroom New Build 2008

Amy Woodgate House Kingston-on-Thames Care Home New Build 2009

Court Farm Road Mottingham Residential Refurbishment 2009

British Estate London Residential and Retail New Build 2009

Newhall Harlow Residential and Retail New Build 2010

Success House London Residential New Build 2010

Castle Hill Primary School Kingston-on-Thames School New Build 2011

Queenshill Estate Leeds Residential New Build 2011

Ferrier Point London Residential Refurbishment 2011

TSB Retrofit for the Future Residential Refurbishment 2012

Edward Woods Estate London Residential Refurbishment 2012

Grove Farm Estate London Residential New Build 2012

Walton Court Centre Aylesbury Mixed Use Refurbishment 2012

2000–2010

3 Sustainability Goes Mainstream

This was the decade during which climate change was finally accepted as a reality. It became impossible for governments to ignore the growing body of evidence for global warming, particularly as the emerging data was also being communicated far more effectively to much wider audiences — through films such as Al Gore's Oscar-winning *An Inconvenient Truth,* for instance. By the end of the decade, barriers to communication had been further eroded by David MacKay's influential book *Sustainable Energy – Without the Hot Air,* which introduced the simple metric 'kWh per person per day' to quantify energy supply and demand. This helped hugely to unravel some of the complexities inherent in the presentation of climate change data.

For those within the wider architectural and building community in the UK, the decade was characterised by the proliferation of advice directed towards them, as institutes and organisations faced up to the incremental tightening of energy performance requirements. By the end of the decade, the building professions were, at last, forced to address climate change, principally through the planning process. Another characteristic of the decade was the promotion of exemplar projects — including many designed by ECD — to the wider industry, as it began to come to terms with the future.

As the decade progressed thermal requirements in the Building Regulations were increased, with revisions to Part L in 2002 and 2006. Meanwhile, the government's 2003 Energy White Paper articulated directions for new energy efficient construction. After much deliberation, the BRE's Ecohomes rating system was superseded, in 2007, by the Code for Sustainable Homes, which rates new housing (only) from levels 1 to 6 — with level 6 representing zero carbon. Prior to this, in December 2006, the Secretary of State for the Environment, Yvette Cooper, announced that, from 2016, all new housing would need to be zero carbon — with incremental improvements to the Building Regulations in 2010 and 2013. At the time of writing, however, an official definition of zero carbon is still awaited.

The European Energy Performance of Buildings Directive (2002) has also begun to have a significant influence, requiring all building owners and landlords to provide an Energy Performance Certificate (EPC) at the point of sale or letting. While not yet imposing overly high standards, the process of calibrating the European building stock in the areas of energy use and efficiency has finally

Phase 3 of the Coopers Road Estate, Success House, provides retail space and 46 flats in a striking six- to eight-storey building on the Old Kent Road.

Left and below right: Perspective views of the South Acton Estate showing the relationship between buildings and public open space.

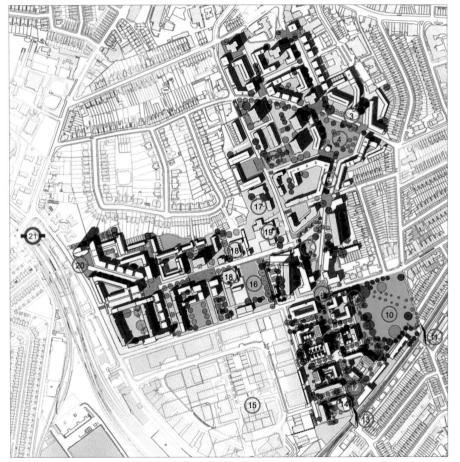

The Urban Design Framework for the proposed area regeneration in and around the South Acton Estate, Ealing.

begun – though, one might argue, still too slowly and with too little emphasis on reporting operational energy usage.

At ECD during the 2000s, we continued to develop our expertise in the housing sector, and the turn of the century found us working on larger regeneration and masterplanning schemes. In 2000, for example, we were appointed by Peabody to work on the regeneration of the Coopers Road Estate in Southwark, south London, developing a masterplan for 250 new homes to be delivered in four phases. Coopers Road has since won a number of design awards and is the subject of a case study in the

publication *Sustainable Urban Design – An Environmental Approach*, edited by Adam Ritchie and Randall Thomas (Taylor and Francis, 2009).

In 2002 we again teamed up with Proctor and Matthews Architects on our largest urban regeneration project to date, the South Acton Estate

A part site section illustrating passive solar strategies for new houses on the Queenshill Estate.

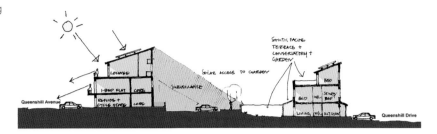

Perspective views of the Queenshill Estate showing the proposed mixture of private and public spaces framed by a variety of new residential properties.

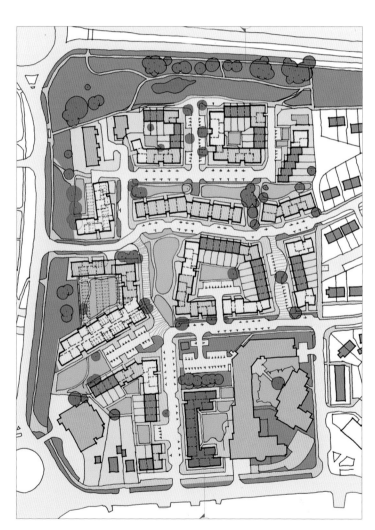

Masterplan of the Queenshill Estate based on streets and squares, with housing and tenure types indicated by different colours.

The north elevation of the noise-attenuating barrier block at the British Estate in Mile End, with south-facing single aspect flats above ground-floor retail units.

An early drawing of the new landscaped entrance court-yard and staircase towers as part of the refurbishment of the Walton Court Centre in Aylesbury, Buckinghamshire.

in Ealing. For this, we jointly produced a comprehensive Urban Design Framework and masterplan for 4000 new homes. Planning permission for the first phase of 650 new-build houses and flats was achieved. Also in London, we are currently involved in a £35-million regeneration programme at the Bede Estate in Mile End, involving both new-build housing and the refurbishment of existing homes.

At the end of the decade this 'sustainable urban regeneration' work is continuing, with the low energy refurbishment of the Walton Court Centre in Aylesbury, for the Vale of Aylesbury Housing Trust.

This is a mixed-use 1970s suburban development containing 'tired' public sector housing, a run-down local shopping centre and failing community facilities. Under the Housing Trust's new management, and with ECD's expertise, the centre will be transformed over the next two years to include both new and refurbished housing, extended and rebuilt community and sports facilities, and new (relocated) shopping facilities. Pedestrian circulation has been rethought and new security arrangements put in place, together with a private courtyard for residents and a new 'high street' of local shops.

Our four-storey mixed use building at Newhall in Harlow, overlooking a key public space.

An early concept sketch of the mews houses at Cliveden Village.

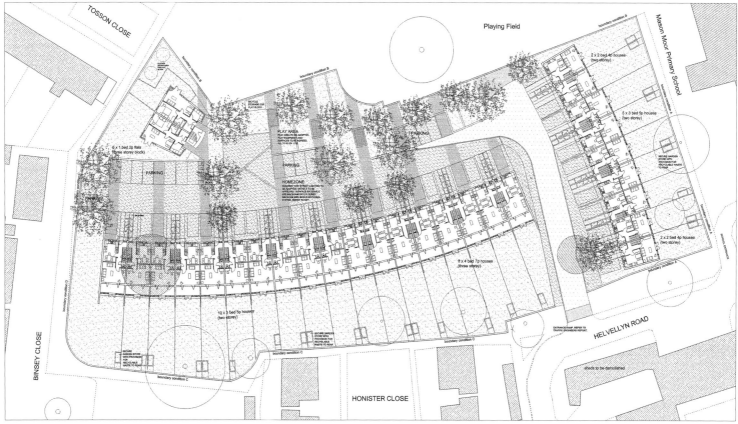

Site plan of the Mason Moor development in Southampton with the housing arranged in two gently curved terraces, facing south and east, and one small block facing west.

At the same time, we are working in Leeds on a phased development of 400 new homes at the Queenshill Estate, to the north of the city centre. The first phase of 58 one and two bedroom 'extra care' homes is due for completion in late 2010.

New-build housing schemes were another feature of the decade. In 2001 the National Trust held a design competition for a residential develop-

ment within the grounds of Cliveden, the Grade 1 Listed country house designed by Sir Charles Barry in the 1850s. ECD and LDA (Landscape Design Associates) teamed up with Countryside Properties to win the competition with a contemporary design based on the concept of the 'kitchen garden'. At Newhall in Harlow we were invited to submit designs for a key site within the masterplan prepared by

Roger Evans Associates. Our four-storey building for 'Plot 1L4' is clad in white render, copper and timber boarding, and contains eight flats and a two-storey live-work unit, over commercial space on the ground floor. The building, which addresses a new public square, was completed in 2009.

Another new-build residential project of this period is Mason Moor in Southampton, a 'Housing Forum' demonstration project for Swaythling Housing Association. The brief demanded homes to "delight tenants and raise their spirits", and we responded with a scheme for 33 timber-frame low energy houses and flats planned around a 'Homezone' access road and featuring a long, curved south-facing terrace of two- and three-storey houses with conservatories. The scheme achieved an EcoHomes rating of Very Good.

In 2002, we were appointed to prepare a masterplan for a large extension to the town of Bude in north Cornwall, on a site that had once

Typical floor plans and section of a two-storey passive solar house at Mason Moor.

The Homezone access road and the two curved terraces at Mason Moor.

Opposite: looking out over the Camel Estuary from the south-facing balcony at the private house in Rock, with its overhanging, solar shading roof.

The environmental strategies employed at Radoon, the private house at Rock in north Cornwall.

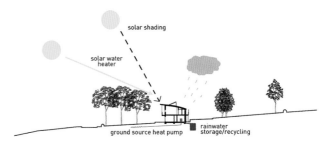

Installation of the ground-source heat exchangers and a rainwater storage tank at Radoon, Rock.

formed part of Broadclose Farm. Also in Cornwall, in 2007, we completed an innovative house in Rock for private clients. This has an 'upside-down' design that provides open-plan living space at first floor level with views over the Camel Estuary. Bedrooms, service and storage areas are located at ground level. The design maximises passive solar gain for heating, while also employing high levels of insulation. Heating and hot water are supplied by a ground source heat pump supplemented by a solar water-heating system, while rainwater is collected and used for WC flushing. One of the features of the design is an overhanging curved roof that shades the south-facing glazing in summer. Combined with stack effect ventilation and heavy thermal mass, this keeps the house comfortably cool in summer.

At the same time, in parallel with our housing work, we continued to expand our sustainable approach into non-domestic sectors, winning several key projects through design competitions. In 1996, for example, we won an RIBA open design competition for a new museum in Banbury, with a

The south elevation of Radoon, located at the top of the site from where it enjoys the best of the views.

Cover of the final report for the RIBA-sponsored Colleges for the Future competition.

Colleges for the Future

RIBA

Right: the bridge gallery linking both sides of the Banbury Museum and *(below)* the timber and render clad extension at Birchensale School.

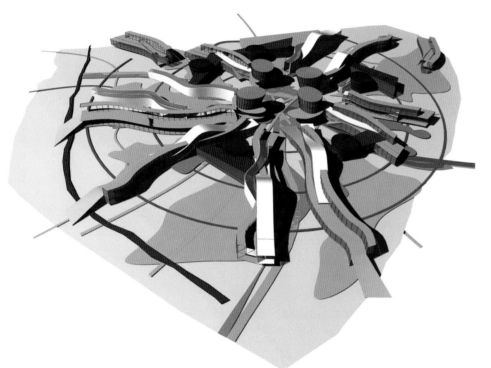

ECD were highly commended in the Colleges for the Future competition, with the judges commenting that our design was "a strong visionary metaphor of ribbons of integrated activity with the college as the natural hub of its locality".

proposal that linked the proposed site's two parts — one on each side of the Oxford Canal — with an 'exhibition gallery' bridge. We subsequently worked closely with the client, Cherwell District Council, to secure Heritage Lottery funding for the project.

In 2000 we were selected, in competition again, to design a new home for the upper school of The Royal Ballet School, as part of a new mixed-use development in Covent Garden, London. Other more recent educational projects have included a major extension to Birchensale School in Redditch and our

'Highly Commended' entry for the RIBA-sponsored Colleges for the Future competition.

At the same time we were successful in winning appointments to design and oversee the building of two extensive industrial and logistics projects in Greenford, west London, as part of the regeneration of a 1930s industrial area. The first was a distribution centre for Scottish and Newcastle Breweries, while the larger was for Entertainment UK (EUK). This has

a floor area of 35,000 square metres — making it ECD's largest building to date — and incorporates office space, a computer centre and a heavily insulated, low energy warehouse, designed to house specialist products at a constant temperature. Now a requirement under the Building Regulations, this was one of the first large buildings in the UK to be tested for air tightness, and it achieved an exceptional level of $3.0\,m^3/hr/m^2$ at 50 Pascal.

One of our more unusual projects at this time came about as the direct result of the expo-

An early design perspective of the Wolseley Sustainable Building Centre, which was completed in 2008.

nential growth in the supply of sustainable materials and products during the second half of the decade – as presaged by the popularity of the annual Ecobuild exhibitions. As part of its push into this burgeoning new marketplace, ECD was appointed by Wolseley UK, one of the largest suppliers of 'green' products in the UK building sector, to design a 'sustainable building centre' at Leamington Spa, Warwickshire. This innovative building, completed in 2008, is in effect a 'living showroom' of sustainable products and systems, all of which are utilised in its design and construction for the purpose of demonstration and promotion.

Another characteristic of the decade was the growth in scope and scale of retrofit projects in the housing sector, in which the existing housing stock is upgraded to significantly improve energy performance. The origins of this area of work for us lay in

A tall central atrium floods the Entertainment UK (EUK) offices with light.

The EUK Headquarters at Greenford, combining offices and computer centre with a large distribution warehouse.

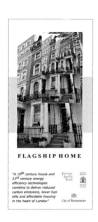

The Flagship Home brochure, outlining plans to refurbish a house on Beaufort Gardens, Kensington, and reduce CO_2 emissions by 60 per cent.

The new secure entrance to Seaton Point with its desk for a full-time concierge.

New brick wall to match existing

New double glazed sash timber window to match existing

New Fifth Floor

Fourth Floor

Third Floor

Second Floor

Restore existing sash windows with new double glazing

First Floor

Ground Floor

Entrance Level

Lower Ground Floor

Total Number of Double Rooms (14 sq m) = 13
Total Number of Single Rooms (11 sq m) = 5
Total Number of WCs = 7 for 31 person

Double Room

Single Room

New Fifth Floor Plan
Double Room

Single Room

Fourth Floor Plan
Double Room

Single Room

Third Floor Plan
Double Room

Single Room

Second Floor Plan
Double Room

Single Room

First Floor Plan
Double Room

Housekeeper Room

Ground Floor Plan

Lower Ground Floor Plan - Self-contained Flat

Details of the low carbon refurbishment of the listed Georgian building in Beaufort Gardens into multi-occupancy studio flats.

small scale energy studies and exemplar projects. In 2002, for example, we undertook a test project for The Royal Borough of Kensington and Chelsea to demonstrate the potential for energy and CO_2 savings in listed properties in central London — for which we prepared a study for a large house in multiple occupation. This led to our involvement in an initiative called 'Flagship Home', where an existing property at 36 Beaufort Gardens was refurbished specifically to deliver significant CO_2 savings — in this instance of around 60 per cent. This was achieved by upgrading the internal and external thermal insulation, fitting double-glazed windows, and adding mechanical ventilation, heat recovery, low energy lighting and solar water heating.

In 2004, for Peabody, we again achieved a 60 per cent reduction in CO_2 emissions from two 13-storey 1950s residential towers at the Roscoe Street Estate in Clerkenwell, London. The energy saving measures included the application of a 200mm thickness of Sto's insulated render to all external walls, and installing new double-glazed windows. A similar approach was taken with the refurbishment of Seaton Point, a 21-storey tower on the Nightingale Estate in Hackney, London.

Later in the decade, in 2009, we undertook another experiment and further pushed the boundaries at Court Farm Road in Mottingham, where we carried out the 'low-carbon' refurbishment of a 1930s mid-terrace house as an exemplar for Hyde Housing Association. By adopting a 'whole house'

Roscoe Towers, Islington, before and after refurbishment.

To reduce heat loss in winter, a glazed outer screen was added to Seaton Point's open balconies.

To help achieve a 60 per cent reduction in CO_2 emissions, the two 1950s-era Roscoe Towers were overclad with 200mm of thermal insulation.

The refurbished Seaton Point (*on the left*) alongside its soon to be demolished neighbour.

A cutaway section showing the low carbon strategies, including solar thermal and PV cells, installed at Court Farm Road, Mottingham.

approach, we were able to cut annual CO_2 emissions by 80 per cent. This was achieved by upgrading the thermal performance of the whole building envelope (including the ground floor, external walls, roof and windows), improving air tightness, installing highly efficient heating and ventilation systems, and integrating renewable energy supplies in the form of solar thermal and roof mounted photovoltaic (PV) cells. A variety of insulation materials were used, including phenolic foam for internal drylining,

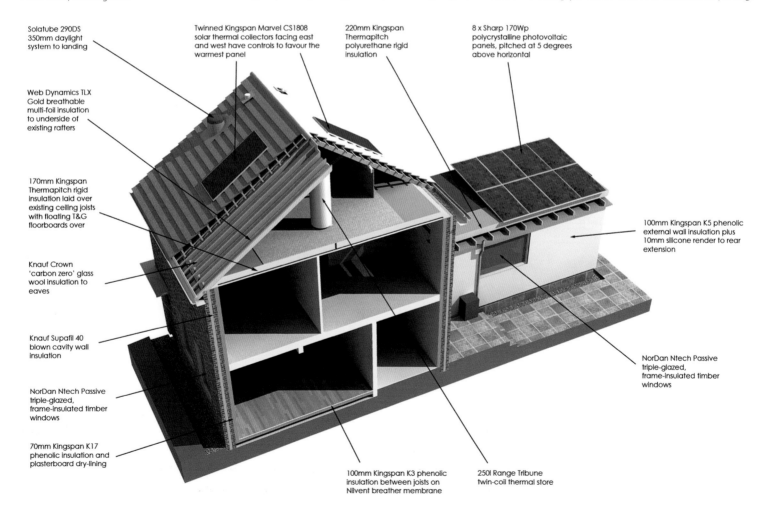

Solatube 290DS 350mm daylight system to landing

Web Dynamics TLX Gold breathable multi-foil insulation to underside of existing rafters

170mm Kingspan Thermapitch rigid insulation laid over existing ceiling joists with floating T&G floorboards over

Knauf Crown 'carbon zero' glass wool insulation to eaves

Knauf Supafil 40 blown cavity wall insulation

NorDan Ntech Passive triple-glazed, frame-insulated timber windows

70mm Kingspan K17 phenolic insulation and plasterboard dry-lining

Twinned Kingspan Marvel CS1808 solar thermal collectors facing east and west have controls to favour the warmest panel

220mm Kingspan Thermapitch polyurethane rigid insulation

8 x Sharp 170Wp polycrystalline photovoltaic panels, pitched at 5 degrees above horizontal

100mm Kingspan K5 phenolic external wall insulation plus 10mm silicone render to rear extension

NorDan Ntech Passive triple-glazed, frame-insulated timber windows

100mm Kingspan K3 phenolic insulation between joists on Nilvent breather membrane

250l Range Tribune twin-coil thermal store

Far left and right: ECD are carrying out the low carbon refurbishment of 13 existing family houses as part of the Technology Strategy Board's Retrofit for the Future programme.

The rear of Court Farm Road showing the highly insulated rear extension topped by PV cells, with a roof mounted solar water heater and rainwater storage butt to supply flushing water for the wcs.

Supplementary heating at Court Farm Road is provided by one of a new range of very efficient gas boilers.

as well as glasswool, polyurethane boards and TLX Gold multi-foil to line the existing rafters and party walls. The windows were replaced with triple-glazed composite units with 'warm edge' spacers.

These measures resulted in an improvement in airtightness from 9.1 to 5.0 m³/hr/m² at 50 Pascal, while CO_2 emissions were further reduced by the installation of a mechanical ventilation and heat recovery system that extracts air from kitchens and bathrooms — reclaiming around 90 per cent of the heat to pre-warm incoming fresh air when required. We also installed LED lighting and low energy white

goods. A programme of monitoring is now under way, recording internal comfort conditions, energy consumption and occupant satisfaction. Court Farm Road has already won a number of awards including 'Sustainable Social Housing Refurbishment Project of the Year' at the Inside Housing Sustainable Housing Awards, 2009.

Following on from this initiative, ECD is now taking a lead role in the government's Retrofit for the Future programme, in which exemplar low-carbon refurbishment and retrofit measures are being installed in sample houses in the social rented sector across the UK. The sample group is largely made up of one-off street properties, and we are responsible for 13 of the 86 dwellings nationwide. We will be testing a variety of technical approaches, mostly using products and systems that are available in the UK marketplace, with some installations developed specifically for the project. All the houses will be monitored over a period of several years by the Energy Saving Trust, in order to identify technically viable solutions for different generic house types.

2010 will also see the completion of two important tower block refurbishment projects, which aim to take renewable energy strategies to new levels. The first, in the Canning Town regeneration area in Newham, London, will see the 23-storey Ferrier Point refurbished as a flagship scheme to 'Decent Homes' standard, with the addition of a high-performance building envelope incorporating

Construction work at Ferrier Point, which is due to be completed in autumn 2010.

Above: Ferrier Point, Newham, before refurbishment and *(right)* a rendering of the finished building which will include PV cladding on the south elevation.

200mm of thermal insulation and triple-glazing. The south elevation will also incorporate 400 square metres of photovoltaic (PV) cells, capable of generating (at peak) 50kW of electricity.

In Shepherd's Bush, work is also under way on extensive upgrades to the three residential tower blocks of the Edward Woods Estate. These will include the largest fully integrated renewable energy systems in London, with 415 square metres of solar PV cells on each tower, as well six 6kW wind turbines. Each tower will also incorporate four super-insulated, low carbon penthouse flats.

A computer generated image of Ferrier Point, including integrated PV cladding on the south facade.

While much attention has been paid to raising standards in new-build housing, ECD has continued to highlight the importance of upgrading the existing stock of buildings. The domestic sector accounts for 27 per cent of the UK's CO_2 emissions but, despite the huge scope to reduce this percentage, there is no funded programme yet in place to take this forward on a sufficiently large scale. Neither, in 2010, are there any overriding legal obligations on homeowners to upgrade their homes to meet important standards. Without legislation in this sector, and without government action to ensure wide-ranging targets are met, real progress remains in the hands of committed professionals like ECD, working alongside equally committed clients.

In the future, all new development will be influenced by the UK Climate Change Act, which became law in November 2008. This legislation, supplemented by the UK Low Carbon Transition Plan, was a major milestone on the route towards a low carbon future. It established a national emissions reduction target of 80 per cent by 2050 (relative to 1990 levels), with an interim reduction target of 26 per cent by 2020. It also required the government to publish five year carbon 'budgets' and report on associated policies and programmes.

The implications are enormous: all new housing will need to be zero carbon by 2016 and all non-domestic buildings by 2019. In line with this, Part L of the Building Regulations (Conservation of Fuel and Power) will be updated in October 2010

A rendering of the Edward Woods Estate, Shepherd's Bush, after refurbishment showing the roof mounted wind turbines and new penthouse flats.

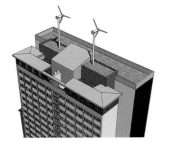

The Edward Woods tower blocks will be fitted with two wind turbines apiece, each capable of supplying 6kW of electricity at peak, and 415 square metres of south-facing PV solar cells.

with the aim of reducing CO_2 emissions in new buildings by a further 25 per cent.

Looking Forward

In 30 years ECD has built over 100 projects and designed many more, in sectors including housing, regeneration, employment, education, arts and leisure. Thirty years of designing and building energy efficient, sustainable buildings has given us a wealth of experience and knowledge. Much of our work has involved technical innovation — we have filled cavities, installed higher performance glazing, integrated conservatories and atrium spaces, reduced air infiltration, tested new heating and thermal storage systems, designed naturally ventilated buildings, installed solar energy systems, monitored performance and evaluated new products and components.

We have learnt that it is important to get the basics right, and to avoid over complex solutions and the excesses of so-called 'eco-bling'. We have also found that agreeing achievable sustainability

targets at the project briefing stage is critical and, as part of this, that it is essential to develop robust and integrated environmental strategies at the concept design stage — when 80 per cent of the key design decisions are made.

Real technical progress has been achieved in our work when we have collaborated with enlightened clients and talented, like-minded professionals from the early stages of the design process. We have been fortunate to work with many excellent engineers, where the building envelope and mechanical services have been developed in a fully integrated way. From this, we have learnt that a high performing building envelope is absolutely key to minimising heating and cooling demands.

As we look forward to the new decade beyond 2010, ECD remains fully committed to its core business of architecture and energy. We relish the challenge of the next 30 years and will strive to make a significant contribution to the necessity of a low carbon society.

Coopers Road Estate

Southwark, London   2001-2010

Below: an artists impression
of a four-storey block of flats
from the street side.

Coopers Road was a failed 1960s housing estate of soulless high-rise blocks and unloved open spaces that Southwark Council, in association with Peabody, decided to redevelop as a model sustainable community.

ECD was appointed to prepare a new masterplan and, working closely with a group of residents, we developed a new

An aerial perspective of the Coopers Road Estate showing the masterplan in its urban context.

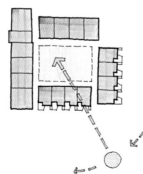

Diagram of a typical courtyard block, with the lower three-storey houses to the south and east to maximise solar penetration into the central space.

layout for the estate based around four courtyards. Each one includes approximately 38 houses and flats – a quantity specifically chosen to strike a balance between protecting privacy and encouraging community life. As a result of the regular monthly meetings that took place throughout the design and construction stages, tenants at Coopers Road have since formed a steering group that continues to promote a strong sense of ownership and civic pride.

A concept sketch exploring some of the early planning ideas in relation to sun angles at different times of the year.

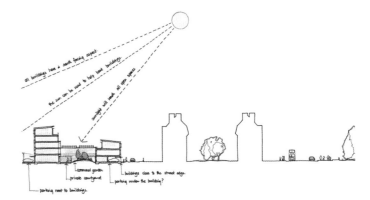

A plan of the estate indicating the four development phases, running in chronological order from green to blue to red to yellow.

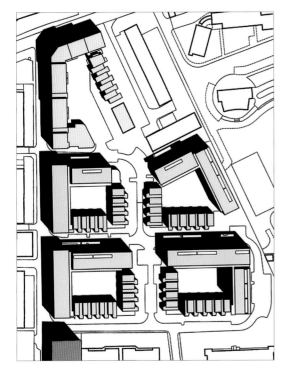

Detail view of a courtyard, showing the potential for the roofs of the larger four-storey blocks to be lined with photovoltaic cells.

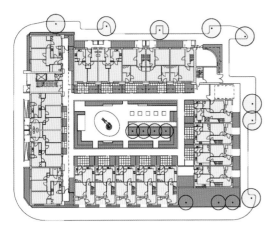

Each of the four courtyards is made up of a mixture of four-storey blocks of flats (purple) and three-storey terrace houses (brown).

Detail views of the elevational treatment of the street facades.

A sectional elevation of one
of the courtyards as built.

A morning view across one
of the landscaped courtyards,
looking towards the four-
storey blocks of flats, here to
the west and north.

The masterplan generates a clear hierarchy of public and private spaces – with communal courtyard gardens providing a secure amenity for people of all ages. Each courtyard is made up of three-storey town houses and four-storey flats and maisonettes, arranged to allow the maximum penetration of sunlight. Access roads are designed as 'Homezones', giving priority to pedestrians and cyclists rather than cars, and car parking is limited to one space for every two dwellings – though this is counterbalanced by ample secure cycle storage in the courtyards.

Thermal insulation standards are in excess of the 2005 Building Regulations and the completed parts of the scheme have already achieved a 'Very Good' Eco-homes rating. A centralised community heating and CHP plant provides heating and hot water, with the electricity generated contributing to the landlord's supplies, in particular the much improved communal lighting. The redevelopment is built to the Lifetime Homes Standard and includes a proportion of homes for shared ownership.

Construction was phased to ensure residents were only required to move once during the redevelopment, with the first phase of 74 dwellings completed in December 2005 and the second, of 80 dwellings, in May 2008. A third phase of

46 flats and maisonettes, a youth club and small retail unit was completed in January 2010 and the final phase is, at the time of writing, at the design stage. Coopers Road has won a number of design awards, including a Civic Trust Commendation in 2006.

Street view of the imposing
sign indicating the entrance
to one of the blocks.

Birchensale Middle School

Redditch, Worcestershire 2002

The completed extension from the south-east, with timber clad classrooms on the first floor floating over a ground floor base of coloured render and dark brickwork.

As a result of demographic changes, in 1998 Worcestershire County Council began a process of rationalising its school buildings in Redditch, leading to ECD being appointed to prepare design proposals for an extension to Birchensale Middle School, which was to be doubled in size from 300 to 600 pupils. The existing building was a SCOLA steel-frame structure from the 1970s, with a high percentage of glazing that meant the building overheated in summer and was too cold in winter.

The brief called for a remodelled entrance, 10 new classrooms, a new multi-purpose hall, and music and laboratory areas. This was a significant addition, but we found that by attaching the new accommodation as a new two-storey wing in front of the school's existing south facade, it was possible to upgrade the thermal performance of the overall envelope sufficiently to allow the original gas boilers to meet the new heating demands.

To optimise internal comfort conditions, careful modelling of the thermal, daylighting and ventilation performance was carried out throughout the design phase, with assistance provided by the *Building Services Journal*'s 'PROBE' (Post-Occupancy Reviews of Buildings and

The ground- and first-floor plans of the extension during three of the five phases of construction, finishing with the completed building.

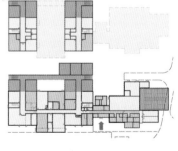

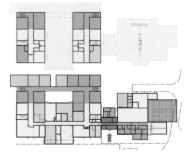

A drawing of the south elevation as built, the building partly sunk into the ground at the eastern end.

Below: galvanised metal grills act as sunshades protecting the new glazed entrance, while inside *(below far right)* circulation areas are, wherever possible, flooded with daylight.

their Engineering) team. Feedback from other recently completed schools was made available to the design team at the briefing/feasibility stage, allowing lessons to be learnt — a procedure adopted by ECD on subsequent school projects. At Birchensale, this resulted in a campaign to encourage staff and pupils to switch off artificial lighting when natural day-lighting levels were adequate.

Construction materials — including western red cedar cladding and areas of

brick and painted render — were selected for their low embodied energy and low maintenance requirements. Completed in September 2002, the building went on to receive a 'Mention' in the 2003 Civic Trust Awards.

Banbury Museum

Banbury, Oxfordshire   2002

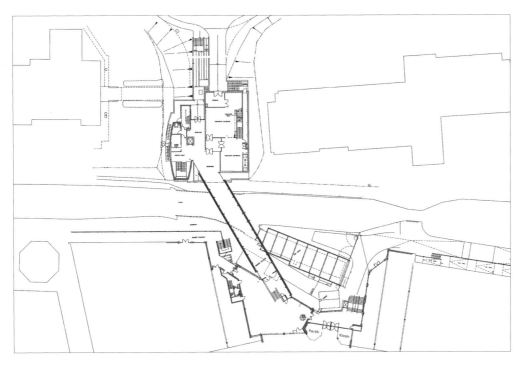

Site plan of Banbury Museum
with the main entrance and
galleries on the north side
of the Oxford Canal, linked by
the gallery bridge to a new
Tourist Information Centre
and Tooley's Boatyard on the
other.

The design brief for this new museum
was challenging because it involved a
site divided into two by the Oxford Canal.
Our response, therefore, consisted of
three main elements: the galleries, a café
and office accommodation on the north
side of the canal; a tourist information
centre and the historic Tooley's Boatyard
(a Scheduled Ancient Monument) on the
south side; and a special bridge gallery
that links the two. Part-funded by the
Heritage Lottery Fund, the project
received significant additional funding
from the client, Cherwell District Council,
who sponsored the competition and the
project jointly with British Waterways.

The project's gallery spaces were
designed to achieve the standards set by
the Museums and Galleries Commission

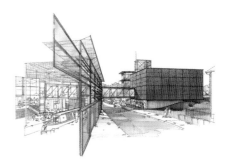

Concept sketch prepared as
part of the competition entry,
with a new glass facade to
Tooley's Boatyard in the foreground.

(now Resource) so that the museum
could, for the first time, receive 'loan'
exhibitions. The standards relate largely
to security issues and environmental

The main entrance to the museum leads into a central reception area, with the main galleries on one side and staff areas and vertical circulation on the other.

Interior views of the main galleries located over the two floors, with the temporary gallery below and the permanent collection above.

Canalside view of museum with the three-storey administration tower of the main block in the foreground and the bridge gallery beyond.

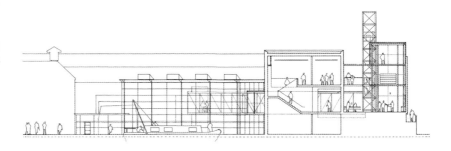

A sectional elevation at concept design stage, with the main galleries and administrative tower in section and the glazed facade to Tooley's Boatyard beyond.

conditions in the galleries, which must preserve the artefacts on display.

To achieve the necessary stable conditions with a low energy approach, the outer facades of the building were highly insulated. In addition, a high mass precast concrete flooring system called Termo-Deck was used in the roof and floors of the gallery block, through which conditioned air passes (via voids in the precast planks) on its way to the gallery spaces. This creates a stable temperature with significantly lower energy use compared with similar lightweight buildings.

The scheme employs simple and complementary architectural forms, clad mainly in white render and terracotta tiles, with full-height glazing to the public areas and the café. Ivor Heal designed the exhibition displays in the museum using complementary materials.

The scheme was completed in 2002 and has proved to be a success in Banbury and beyond, with visitor numbers far exceeding predictions.

Above: an internal view of the bridge gallery and *(right)* an early sectional elevation of the museum.

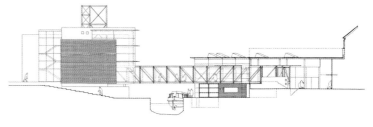

A view of the museum from the towpath with the re-housed Tooley's Boatyard on the left.

The Royal Ballet School

Covent Garden, London   2002

The Long Acre elevation, with four storeys of student facilities and classrooms over retail space on the ground floor, and the top floor set back to mirror the surrounding mansard roofs.

This project came about in 1999, when The Royal Ballet School (RBS) decided to relocate its upper school from Barons Court, West London, to a site next to The Royal Opera House in Covent Garden. The new building occupies a tight urban site incorporating three listed buildings, and provides five bright daylit dance studios stacked in two 'piles', one beside the other.

The public access areas, teaching rooms, offices and storage space are wrapped around two sides of the core of studios, with the main entrance tucked into the Floral Street frontage. The ballet school premises are located at first floor and above, while ground and basement levels are occupied by 1200 square metres of retail space — currently a Zara store. The building was constructed as a single project under one contract.

The main entrance off Floral Street, a bright but modest space leading to a reception area deep in the heart of the building.

The Floral Street elevation with the main entrance and its four-metre high feature 'sign' in the foreground, and the six projecting oak windows of the main dance studios beyond.

THE ROYAL BALLET SCHOOL

There are five dance studios in all, two overlooking Floral Street and three set into the heart of the building, but lit with windows overlooking a central lightwell.

The main double-height foyer at the first floor, the social heart of the building leading directly to dance studios on one side and to student facilities and smaller classrooms beyond.

The floor plans illustrating how the building had to be carefully slotted into a tight urban site while retaining existing buildings in two opposing corners.

KEY
1 entrance
2 reception
3 staff offices
4 visitors reception
5 staff changing
6 de Valois studio
7 Linden studio
8 boys' changing room
9 student common room
10 staff common room
11 Princess Margaret studio
12 Dowell/Sibley studio
13 girls' changing room
14 physiotherapy
15 gym
16 body conditioning
17 pianists room
18 Djanogly studio
19 classroom
20 first aid
21 wardrobe
22 audio visual room

Presentation drawing of the east elevation, with the tall bulk of the studios hidden behind a cloak of student facilities and teaching spaces overlooking Hanover Place.

The complex site is located in a Conservation Area and is adjoined by several buildings in multiple ownership, complicating the Rights of Light issues. Also, the Piccadilly tube line passes below, which had major implications for the structural design. In addition, a full archaeological dig of the whole site was required, which meant that the existing buildings had to be supported during the excavations. However, an unusual Saxon jewelled brooch was found, which now resides in the Museum of London.

External treatment varies between elevations. On Floral Street, above the stone cladding of the retail frontage, large box-framed windows are set into a brick elevation, reflecting the scale of the studios within. The ballet school's entrance is marked by a four-metre-high projecting steel and glass feature, while in Hanover Place glass-faced display cases incorporated into the facade publicise the work of the school. The north elevation is dominated more by the retail element of the scheme, as well as two of the Grade 2 Listed buildings that form part of the development.

The scheme was completed in 2002, with the school's interior fittings and finishes by the Westwood Partnership.

One of the double-height dance studios brightly lit by tall windows overlooking the central lightwell.

Daylight in the top floor studio is supplemented by a single rooflight.

Broadclose Farm

Bude, Cornwall 2006

Concept sketch for a typical two-storey house, finished in a mixture of slate, timber boarding and render.

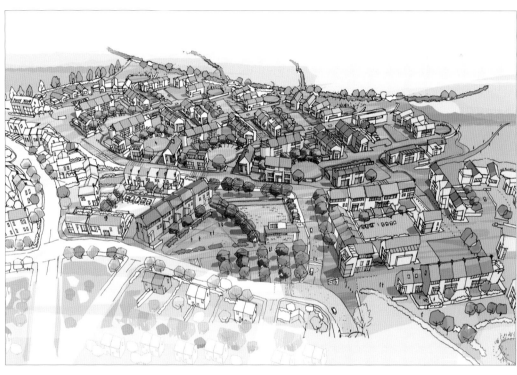

Aerial perspective of the site illustrating its relationship to the edge of Bude and the open countryside beyond.

The housing density on the site is low, allowing significant areas of landscaping between the houses, which are grouped in clusters.

In 2002, we were approached by LDA (Landscape Design Associates) to collaborate on a masterplan for a new mixed-tenure housing development on the eastern edge of Bude in north Cornwall. The focus of the brief was a 7-hectare site — on land formerly belonging to Broadclose Farm — situated between the communities of Bude, Stratton and Flexbury, immediately adjacent to a new supermarket. We were asked to test the capacity of the site for residential development, win the support of local communities, and to provide a regional exemplar of sustainability in social, economic and environmental terms.

Before developing our proposals, we undertook a detailed investigation of the local context, analysing the surrounding landscape, ecology, footpaths, transport and views, and assessing the local facilities and services infrastructure. At the same time we launched an extensive programme of consultation with the local residents' associations to identify issues of concern within the local community. Emerging high on the list of priorities were the need to establish a sense of place and arrival, to make streets pedestrian-friendly and to provide dedicated play spaces for children.

The resulting masterplan incorporates 183 new homes in a 'pepper potted'

The detailed design of the houses was carried out by the Trewin Design Partnership and follows the concept sketches closely.

Access roads were carefully planned to allow plenty of generous, pedestrian friendly open areas where children can play in complete safety.

arrangement, made up of housing for private sale and social rent with no visual distinction between the two. The layout is based on a series of housing clusters that are designed to maximise solar gain while responding to the north-facing slope of the site. Access roads are traffic-calmed and designed as 'Homezones'. In planning terms, the housing along the site's northern boundary creates a positive 'edge' to the development, reinforcing its containment and sense of identity.

The architectural treatment is a modern interpretation of traditional Cornish materials — render and slate, with small areas of shiplap timber cladding. External spaces are clearly defined as either 'public' or 'private' and the landscaping incorporates traditional Cornish dry stone walls. The detail design for the scheme was developed by the Trewin Design Partnership. It was completed in 2006 and won the Richard Feilden Housing Design Award in 2007.

Cliveden Village

Taplow, Buckinghamshire 2007

Early concept sketch of the three-storey apartment buildings at the edge of the site, looking out towards the surrounding woodland.

This scheme of new housing is set on an escarpment above the River Thames within the Grade 1 Listed grounds of Cliveden House. The 6.5-hectare site was formerly occupied by the Canadian Red Cross Memorial Hospital, which closed in 1986 and was subsequently demolished, leaving a brownfield site suitable for redevelopment. Lying some distance from the main house, the site slopes gently to the south and is completely enclosed by mature oak and beech trees, giving it a contained and secluded feel.

The layout of 71 houses and 64 apartments (for sale to the over 55s) is formal and orthogonal, responding to the predominant north-south axis of the site. The two- and three-storey houses face south to maximise passive solar gain, while the three-storey apartments form an edge along the site's western boundary.

Externally, natural materials have been used to express the aspirations of a 'sustainable community', with the apartments clad in sandstone and the houses in an earth-coloured Monocouche render system. Natural slate is used for the pitched roofs and the rainwater pipes and gutters are in copper. The simple yet formal landscape design employs high-quality materials to define the communal open spaces, while internally, generous space standards allow light and airy rooms, with balconies for every apartment.

A strong environmental agenda ensured that every dwelling is well insulated, while each of the mechanical ventilation systems has been fitted with efficient heat recovery units. Heating is

A variety of sustainable energy efficiency measures were explored, including rainwater collection, the on-site treatment of waste water and a combined gas/biofuel CHP to supply heat and electricity. Not all proposals made it to the final scheme.

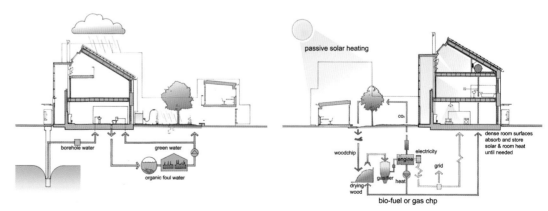

A terrace of south-facing, two-storey houses close to the edge of the site, with mature woodland beyond.

The original ECD site plan, with its mixture of houses and terraces laid out around elegantly landscaped mews, streets, courtyards and open spaces. The final scheme was developed for construction by Countryside Properties with Onko Architects.

by condensing gas boilers and the south-facing houses use integrated solar water heating systems. Materials were sourced locally wherever possible and all timber was FSC accredited. Low energy lighting is used in most spaces, kitchen appliances are 'A' rated and dual flush WCs have been installed. Segregated

recycling facilities are provided, and each property is fitted with a green waste system that is operated in conjunction with the National Trust.

The scheme achieved an Ecohomes 'Excellent' rating and has won a number of awards including a Building for Life 'Gold' standard.

A concept sketch of one of the terraces, set well back from the road behind an avenue of trees.

A terrace of houses along the northern boundary of the site, with solar water heaters on the roof and fixed timber louvres shading the south-facing windows from the summer, but not winter, sun.

Though located on the Cliveden Estate, Cliveden Village is hidden from the House by the natural fall of the land and the extensive woodland on every side.

Night time view of a terrace of mews houses, terminating with a copper-clad three-storey residence matching the scale of the apartment buildings opposite.

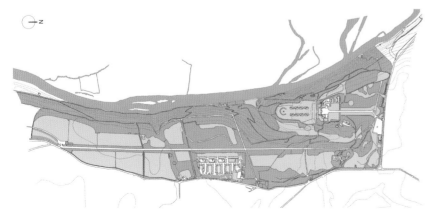

Wolseley Sustainable Building Centre

Leamington Spa, Warwickshire   2008

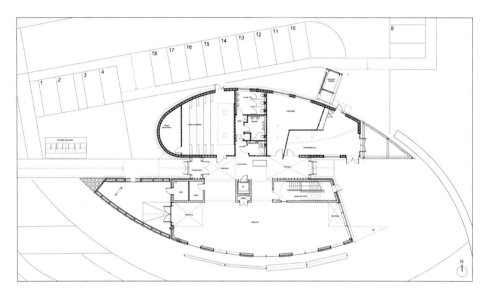

Ground floor plan showing the north and south zones, separated by the central top-lit access spine.

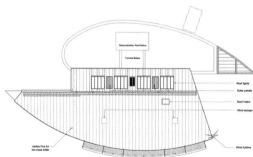

Roof plan with solar collectors located along the central spine and a demonstration sedum roof on the north wing.

Wolseley UK is a major supplier of building materials who, confronted with a growing stock of 'sustainable' materials and products, decided to build a showroom to inform their customers. The initial brief was very loosely defined, calling for a building of 600 to 700 square metres over two floors, to be built on the Wolseley headquarters 'campus' outside Leamington Spa.

Appointed lead designer for the project in January 2005, ECD identified a location in the south-east corner of the site, where the building would have unobstructed solar access and maximum public exposure. Following discussions with the client, a design evolved with distinct north and south wings separated by a central circulation spine.

The challenge was to incorporate a broad range of (sustainable) materials and components in a coherent and aesthetically pleasing manner, while expressing the principles of sustainable design. Our solution deliberately juxtaposed two alternative approaches to low-energy design, with the south wing taking a heavy thermal mass approach, that utilises passive solar gain in winter and external shading and natural ventilation in summer. The north wing, by contrast, has a more organic form and is built in lightweight engineered timber.

Above right: the south elevation with its full-height glazing shaded by a fixed *brise-soleil* and *(below right)* the contrasting timber-clad wing on the north elevation.

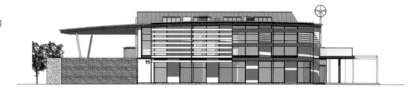

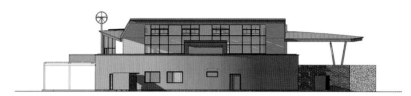

A view of the building from the north-west shortly after completion, before the final landscaping had taken hold.

The east elevation with the two wings separated by the fully glazed central spine.

View of the building from the south-east, contrasting the heavy thermal mass construction of the two-storey south wing with the engineered timber structure of the north.

The layout promotes a visitor route that flows easily from the entrance to an audio-visual presentation, then on to demonstration galleries on ground and first floors, including a roof terrace where visitors can see sedum roofing, sun pipes, solar PV roof tiles and solar thermal systems at close hand. On the ground floor there are working examples of a condensing gas boiler, ground source heat pump and biomass boiler.

Since its completion in June 2008, the centre has been in continuous use promoting Wolseley's products to a wide range of organisations. The building achieved a 'bespoke' BREEAM rating (as a non-conventional building) of Excellent, and has won many awards, including the Edie Award for Best Sustainable Construction Project and the ICE West Midlands Innovation Award, both in 2008.

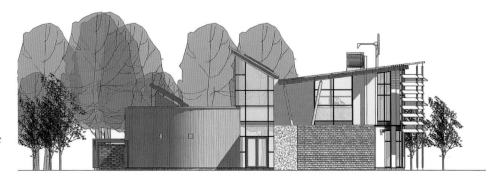

A presentation drawing of the west elevation, all but identical to the finished building.

Right: the upper level of the central spine looking out over the sedum roof on the north wing and *(far right)* exposed services on display in the south wing.

The west elevation looking towards the main entrance from the car park, displaying some of the company's products and materials.

Appendices

Postscript
by Koen Steemers

Koen Steemers

30:30 Vision

Buildings consume more energy now than 30 years ago. I'm not referring here to the cutting-edge low energy buildings of ECD, but to the overall building stock in a climate of change.

In 1980 the annual energy demand for UK housing, which accounts for around 30 per cent of the UK's total energy use, stood at 40 million tonnes of oil equivalent (mtoe). Today the figure is nearly 50 mtoe. The only positive spin on this, apart from the emergence of individual innovative exemplar projects, is that the 'dash for gas' has stemmed the CO_2 emissions associated with this increasing energy demand.

Despite this, the underlying question remains: why are we using more energy now? The answer is in part associated with population increase, although the statistics show that the energy demand per person has also been rising (from 0.7 toe/person to 0.8 toe/person). The second part of the answer is that the energy increase is attributable to the increasing number of households, rising from 20 million to 25 million over the period, due to demographic changes such as an aging population and increasing divorce rates, with the net result that household sizes are decreasing.

When we allow for these two key demographic factors, the annual energy demand in most British homes has remained largely unchanged over the past 30 years, holding steady at about 2 toe per household.

During this period we have seen an increasing awareness of energy issues, initially triggered by the first major oil crisis of 1973/74, and the introduction of energy-related building regulations related to reducing heating loads — which account for around 60 per cent of domestic energy demand. As a result, the use of wall insulation has risen from 2 per cent in 1974 to 37 per cent in 2004, and the application of double glazing has increased from 8 to 83 per cent over the same period.

So why has energy demand not reduced? The simple answer is people. A number of occupant-related factors have counteracted the technological advances made. The enlightened clients and users of ECD's buildings work with their architects to understand and achieve environmental goals. The wider population has the new energy standards imposed upon them and tend to exploit the opportunities that these provide. The most obvious of these is increasing comfort: the average household temperature in 1980 was 14°C, whereas today this average is 20°C. This increased comfort standard — where more rooms are warmed to a higher temperature, even in the existing and poorly insulated building stock — would have resulted in a doubling of the energy demand if it had not been for the much improved thermal characteristics of the newer buildings.

Improved thermal comfort has gone hand-in-hand with increased space standards — smaller households having resulted in an increased floor

The original 'Passivhaus' in Darmstadt, Germany, pointing the way towards new 'super insulated' airtight construction methods for northern Europe.

area per person – and the growing use of appliances as a result of greater disposable income. Energy efficiency has thus delivered improved standards of life rather than reduced energy use. A similar trend can be observed in non-domestic buildings, where increased comfort expectations have made the use of energy-intensive air conditioning increasingly the norm, stimulated in part by the ubiquitous use of air conditioning in hotels, cars, restaurants, and so on. Air-conditioned offices on average consume more than twice the energy use per square metre of naturally ventilated offices. Along with this fact there is also increasing evidence that when we model our non-domestic building designs to predict the energy use, we often fail to anticipate occupant behaviour and their interface with control systems, resulting sometimes in a 2:1 discrepancy between measured and predicted performance.

To date, our energy efficiency policies have managed to stem an increase in the energy demand of buildings, but have not yet managed to reduce overall energy use, primarily as a result of what can broadly be summarised as 'human agency'. However, there are individual cases, such as with ECD and their clients, where common aspirations and early engagement have led to low energy buildings and, crucially, low energy users.

The Next 30 Years

The context for the next 30 years is challenging: the climate is changing, the population is increasing (globally from 6.8bn to 8.6bn, and in the UK from 62m to 74m) and becoming older. Living standards, particularly in China and India, will increase rapidly, resulting in a continuation of the trends outlined above. In the UK and elsewhere, a concern is that householders will turn to domestic air conditioning during the anticipated hot spells, counteracting any theoretical advantages of reduced heating demand due to global warming. Indeed, the air-conditioning industry is already targeting the perceived potential of the lower end of the market, with domestic air-conditioning units now widely available at your local DIY store in the summer.

A huge refurbishment action, demanding war-time effort, is required to tackle the 'backlog' of existing, poorly performing buildings, if we are to achieve the ambitious UK emissions targets of 80 per cent below 1990 levels by 2050. We can learn from vernacular architecture in southern Europe to avoid overheating — for example, by the use of thermal mass and shutters — and from northern Europe, where high levels of insulation and the use

of earth sheltering to reduce ventilation heat loss is the tradition. Perhaps more importantly, we need to design and inhabit buildings in an adaptable way, not just to respond to changing seasons but also changing lifestyles, expectations and work habits. The term 'long life, loose fit, low energy' still resonates, although it was first coined in 1972 — before the oil crisis of 1973/74 — by the then President of the RIBA, Alex Gordon.

The challenges and opportunities are now bigger than the design of single buildings, despite — and in part because of — the UK Government's target of 'zero carbon' new homes from 2016 and new non-domestic buildings from 2019. In total, buildings and ground transport account for three-quarters of the UK's energy demand. This means that the way we design cities, including transport infrastructure and renewable energy sources, has to be integrated and holistic.

An Academic's Perspective

The emphasis of academic research has shifted over the last 30 years and has arguably been a precursor to changes in the practice of sustainable design. When I first started studying architecture at Bath University 30 years ago, and 'cut my teeth' as an architectural assistant at ECD in the mid 1980s, there was limited interest in energy efficiency in academia. A hard-core group of teachers and practitioners — including Peter Clegg and Derek Croome at Bath University, and David Turrent and Nick Baker

at ECD — confirmed for me that energy in architecture was a creative and valuable pursuit.

Alongside technical criteria and targets, environmental design is increasingly presented in terms of sensory and experiential design. Key precursors to this are Steen Eiler Rasmussen's *Experiencing Architecture* (1959) and Lisa Heschong's *Thermal Delight in Architecture* (1979), but more recently this momentum has been accelerated with books such as *Environmental Diversity in Architecture* (2004), Juhani Pallasmaa's *The Eyes of the Skin: Architecture and the Senses* (2005) and Dean Hawkes' *The Environmental Imagination* (2008).

The issues of sustainability are increasingly reflected in Government priorities and new directions for practitioners, with a focus on planning for low carbon development in the context of climate change. Architecture, renewable energy, community, jobs, infrastructure, adaptation and mitigation are now often discussed in the same document. In the next 30 years we need to take up these challenges — meeting technical targets while designing better spaces for people, with an emphasis on neighbourhoods and cities rather than one-off buildings. And it is my expectation that ECD will be leading the way.

Koen Steemers
Professor of Sustainable Design and
Head of the Department of Architecture,
University of Cambridge

The Office

We have enjoyed the privilege of working with many talented architects, designers and energy and environmental experts at ECD over the last 30 years. We include here the names of those currently working at ECD, as well as those who have worked with us in the past. In compiling the 'Staff Past' list, we have trawled through our memories and records, and consulted several previous members of ECD. We hope the list is comprehensive and extend our apologies to anyone we may have missed. To one and all, our sincere thanks.

Richard and David

The London team in the new
ECD office in Bermondsey,
London, 2008.

Staff Past

Jorge Amezcua
Dave Andrews
Catherine Arotsky
Mark Atkinson
Miles Attenborough
Mark Auvray
Selcuk Avci
Darren Ayres

Austin Baggett
Nick Baker
Nitin Bansal
Anne Barwick
Edward Beardsmore
Halima Begum
Rafe Bertram
Amolak Singh Bhooi
David Billingham
Darren Bland
Claudia Bloom
Mark Blythen
Andrew Borley
Catherine Brick
Jacqui Brown
Michael Buckley
Simon Burton
Renata Byrne

David Cannell
Sean Carpenter
Sam Castling
Ronald Chan
Marco Columbo
Nicola Coulston

Nigel Craddock
Andy Crawford
Alison Crompton
Andy Cullen
Ben Cunliffe

Chris Dalberg
Sara Darwin
Jim Davidson
Reuben Davies
Simon Davies
Andrew Day
Lionel Delorme
Azita Dezfouli
John Doggart
Simon Dove
Oliver Driscoll

Kevin Edmunds
Jo Edwards

Vivien Fairlamb
John Field
Mark Fineberg
Loic Finlan
Graham Finlay
Adam Firth
Peter Fisher
Joy-Ann Fleming
Brian Ford
Charlotte Forfieh
Jorn Frenzel

Andrew Gardener
Simon Gathercole
Ramiro Godoy
Clare Goldenberg
Andrew Goodwin
Zac Grant
David Graves
Tom Gresford

Robert Hagan
Mark Hall
Jim Harrison
Rebecca Hassett
Simon Hay
Henriette Helstrup
Malgorzata Hendzel
Ian Hogan
Gillian Holland
Alan Horton
Ann Hutchinson

Sidonia Immler
Rosemary Ind

Nathan James
Sarah Jefferson
Simon Johns
Ray Jones

Gail Kenton
Sofia Kesidou
Simon King
Kenan Klico
Ming-Wa Ko
Marcin Kolakowski

Pam Kovachich
Barbara Kuit

John Lancaster
Gary Lawrence
Rachel Leggett
Yuan Lin
Nick Lloyd
Tony Lucas
Steve Lyman

Jes Mainwaring
Sara Mason
John Maxwell
Danielle McCartney
Alison McDonald
Steve McGill
Andrew Mellor
Azzy Mohammad
Jane Monahan
Vaila Morrison
Marianne Muller
Emma Munden
David Mundow
Simon Mundy
Adriette Myburgh

Mark Newey
Robin Newington
Bridget Nicholson
Paul Nicholson
Jennifer Nilsson
Anushe Nizam

James Oliver
Brendan O'Neill
Tadj Oreszczyn

Jay Patel
Riku Patokoski
Belinda Piovesan
David Pleasants
Vinesh Pomal
Dorothy Pontin
John Pratley
Mike Priaulx

Scott Radburn
Kim Randall
Tom Randall
Simon Rayner
Yotan Reich
David Rhodes
Caitriona Riain
Michael Ridden
Peter Roberts
Colin Robertson
Hannah Routh
Bill Rowe
Paul Ruff

Ian Sang
Lucy Savanis
Michael Schimmel-
    schmidt

Guy Shackle
Barry Shaw
Niall Skehan
John Smart
Ben Smith
Nick Sommerville
Soong Shu Kong
Colin Speer
Mike Spike
Andrew Stainsby
Katy Steele
Koen Steemers
Sarah-Jane Stewart
Peter Stokes
Lynne Sullivan

Phillippa Thomas
Mark Thomasson
Mark Thompson
Jamie Tillotson
Jonathan Tivey
Joel Trindade

Keyer Vadodaria
Xavier Valladores
Susan Venner
Paul Vick

George Wachnicki
Rachel Waggett
Geoff Wain
James Walker
Richard Wallis

Acknowledgements

Michelle Wangusi
Peter Warm
Pratima Washan
Sarah Watlinson
Norman Webber
Steve Whitehill
Tim Wilcockson
James Wild
Julian Williams
Sue Wolff
Juliet Wood
Jo Wreford
Richard Wyn-Davies

Robert Young

Artur Zontek
Suzie Zuber

Special thanks go to Ian Lambot for his patience and tenacity in getting this book produced, to Katrina Thomas for assistance with the images, and to Ellie Duffy of Duffy Design for her help with the text.

We also thank Dominic Michaelis to whom this book is dedicated, for his support and encouragement when we were students and young architects at the start of this journey.

Looking at the contributions made to ECD's work over the past 30 years, it's hard and perhaps unfair to pick out individuals for special mention, as so many people have given willingly of their time, commitment, knowledge and talents. But particular thanks are due to several architects who were former Partners and Associates. In chronological order, we include here Jes Mainwaring, David Billingham, Jo Wreford, Lynne Sullivan, Tony Lucas, Paul Nicholson, Selcuk Avci, Kenan Klico, Sara Darwin, Juliet Wood, Brendan O'Neill, Peter Stokes and Suzie Zuber.

From the energy consultancy side of the practice we give special thanks to John Doggart, co-founder of ECD, and particular thanks to former Associates Ramiro Godoy, Nick Baker, Simon Burton, Tadj Oreszczyn, Miles Attenborough and Alison Crompton.

We also acknowledge the substantial creative and technical contributions made to ECD's work by other external consultants, who are too numerous to credit here in full. These include engineers and technical advisers of numerous disciplines, landscape architects, planning consultants and many other individuals. Again, sincere thanks to all involved.

In 2010 David and Richard remain as Directors of both ECD Architects (the architectural practice) and ECD Project Services (the energy consultancy). In 2009 they were joined by Ian Sarchett as Managing Director.

In addition to the many talented professionals in the office today, the Directors are very ably supported by three Associate Directors in London, namely Mark Elton (Head of Sustainability), John Moakes and James Traynor, and one Associate, Dan Jenkins. ECD recently opened a Glasgow office which is looked after by Directors David Fisher and Alan Campbell, with Associate Alistair Cameron.

ECD Project Services is the specialist energy consultancy arm of the practice, headed by Michael Birnie.

In 2007 ECD joined forces with the multi-disciplinary consultancy firm, Keegans, working within a group structure, through which ECD is supported by N-Able Group directors Danny Innes, Luke Coombs and Colette McHugh.

Awards

2010

ECD Architects
Sustainable Housing Awards
Shortlisted: Consultancy of the Year — *for Sustainable Social Housing design/construction*
Wolseley Sustainable Building Centre, Leamington Spa, Warwickshire
Leamington Society Awards
Winner: Notable New Buildings and Conservation Award

2009

Court Farm Road, Mottingham, London
National Home Improvement Council
Winner: The George Plucknett Award
Winner: The Big Green Home Award
Inside Housing Sustainable Housing Awards
Winner: Sustainable Social Housing Refurbishment Project of the Year
Sustain Magazine Awards
Shortlisted: Design & Architecture Award for Refurbishment
Wolseley Sustainable Building Centre, Leamington Spa, Warwickshire
Sustain Magazine Awards
Shortlisted: Design & Architecture Award for Construction

2008

British Estate, Mile End, London
Your New Home Awards
Winner: Best City Development
Charette Masterplan
Winner: Living Steel Extreme Housing Competition
Coopers Road Estate, Southwark, London
CABE Awards
Winner: Building for Life Silver Standard

ECD Jigsaw House
The Mail on Sunday British Homes Awards
Finalist: Tomorrow's Lifestyle Home Design Competition
Wolseley Sustainable Building Centre, Leamington Spa, Warwickshire
Edie Awards for Environmental Excellence
Winner: Best Sustainable Construction Project
Institute of Civil Engineers Awards, West Midlands
Winner: Innovation Award

2007

Broadclose Farm, Bude, Cornwall
Housing Design Awards
Winner: Richard Feilden Award
(masterplan by ECD Architects, implemented by Trewin Design Partnership)
Coopers Road Estate, Southwark, London
ASC Awards for Sustainable Communities
Finalist: Well Designed and Well Built Category
Radoon, Rock, Cornwall
Green Apple Awards
Winner: National Silver in Residential Category

2006

Coopers Road Estate, Southwark, London
Commendation: Civic Trust Award

2004

Children's Centre Project
Winner: RIBA Competition
Colleges for the Future
Commendation: RIBA/LSC Colleges for the Future Competition
Coopers Road Estate, Southwark, London
Shortlisted: HBF/WWF Sustainable New Homes Award

2003

Banbury Museum, Banbury, Oxfordshire
Long list: The Gulbenkian Prize for Museums and Galleries

Birchensale Middle School, Redditch, Worcestershire
Mention: Civic Trust Award

2001

Wetlands Conservation Centre, Slimbridge, Gloucestershire
Winner: Civic Trust Award

2000

Wetlands Conservation Centre, Slimbridge, Gloucestershire
Wycliffe Shield Awards
Winner: Design with special consideration for the benefit of people with disabilities

1999

Royal Holloway, University of London, Egham, Surrey
Winner: RIBA Regional Architecture Awards

Templeton College, Oxford, Oxfordshire
Winner: Vale of White Horse Design Award

Zero CO_2 Housing, Newark-on-Trent, Nottinghamshire
Winner: DETR sponsored RIBA competition

1997

Silchester Estate, Kensington, London
Winner: Disability Access Awards – *for the Disability Resource Centre*

1996

ECD Architects
Premier Award: Business Commitment to the Environment

Banbury Museum, Banbury, Oxfordshire
Winner: RIBA Design Competition

Linacre College, Oxford, Oxfordshire
Winner: Green Building of the Year

Queen's Building, Anglia Ruskin University, Essex
Highly Commended: Green Building of the Year

1993

International Garden Festival, Stuttgart, Germany
UK Winner: Experimental ecological house competition

1990

Salehurst School, Robertsbridge, East Sussex
Winner: BETA Regional Award – Seeboard Region
(as Building Services and Energy Consultant)

1989

Lamerton Street, Deptford, London
Building Industry Convention Awards
Winner: ARC Award for Low Energy Housing

Spectrum 7, Milton Keynes, Buckinghamshire
Building Industry Convention Awards
Winner: The Pilkington Award for Low Energy Commercial Buildings

'Working in the City' Sustainable Office
Special Mention: CEC 'Working in the City' Competition

1988

Cromartie Road, Islington, London
Winner: RIBA Energy Efficiency Awards

1986

Shakespeare School, Eastleigh, Hampshire
CIBS/RIBA/RICS Energy in Buildings Awards
Winner: Non-domestic Sector *(as Building Services and Energy Consultant)*

Clients

Affinity Sutton Group
Aldwyck Housing Association
Anglia Ruskin University
Apollo Group

BBC Money Programme
Beaver Housing Society
Berkeley Square Properties
BICC Group
Boston Haven Developments
Botes Construction
BRE Conservation Support Unit
Bride Hall Developments
British Gas
British Standards Institute
Broseley Homes
Building Research Establishment

Chancerygate Properties
Chancery St James
Charterfield Asset Management
Cherwell District Council
Chichester Diocesan Housing
  Association
CHISEL Neighbourhood Housing
  Association
Circle 33 Housing Trust
  (Circle Anglia)
City of Stuttgart
City of Westminster
CityWest Homes
Commission of the European
  Communities (European Union)

Commonwealth Science Council
Copper Development Association
Countryside Properties
Crawley Homes

Department of the Environment
Dolphin Square Foundation
Dove Brothers (Laing O'Rourke)
Durkan Group
Durtnell Construction

Ealing Family Housing Association
  (Catalyst Housing Group)
EastendHomes
Eastern Electricity
East London Housing Association
East Sussex County Council
East Thames Housing Group
Energy Conscious Homes
Energy Efficiency Office
  (Department of Energy)
Energy Park Developments
Energy Technology Support Unit
  (Department of Energy)
Enfield Homes
English Partnerships
Entertainment UK
Essex County Council

Galliard Homes
Galliford Try
Goldsmiths College, London
Guinness Trust

H&F Homes
Hastoe Housing Association

Hampshire County Council
Higgins Homes
Hughes Homes
Hyde Housing Group

Islington Community Housing
  Co-operative

Keegans Group
Kensington Housing Trust
  (Catalyst Housing Group)
Kent County Council
Kitewood Estates

Laing Homes
Land Securities
Lebuc Holdings
Leeds Jewish Housing Association
Linacre College, Oxford
Linford Wood Developments
Liverpool Housing Action Trust
London Borough of Camden
London Borough of Croydon
London Borough of Hackney
London Borough of Hammersmith
  and Fulham
London Borough of Lambeth
London Borough of Lewisham
London Borough of Newham
London Borough of Southwark
London Borough of Tower Hamlets
London Borough of Waltham Forest

London Docklands Development
    Corporation
London and Quadrant Housing
    Trust

Manhattan Loft Corporation
Mansell Construction
Metropolitan Housing Trust
Meyer Family Trust
Milton Keynes Development
    Corporation
Milton Keynes Housing Association
    (Midsummer Housing Association)

National Energy Foundation
National Housing Federation
Network Housing Group
Newhall Properties
North British Housing Association
    (Places for People)
North Cornwall District Council
Notting Hill Housing Trust
Nottingham Trent University

Oakes Trust
Old Ford Housing Association
    (Circle Anglia)
Open University

P&O Properties
Peabody

Reading Borough Council
Regalian Properties
Ripley Village Hall Development
    Committee

Rockwool Insulation
Royal Borough of Kensington and
    Chelsea
Royal Borough of Kingston upon
    Thames
Royal Holloway, University of
    London

SE Land
S&S Homes
Salmon Developments
Salmon Harvester Properties
Samuel Lewis Housing Trust
    (Southern Housing Group)
Scottish Homes (Sanctuary
    Scotland Housing Association)
Scottish and Newcastle
Society for Co-operative Dwellings
Southdale Homes
South London Family Housing Asso-
    ciation (Horizon Housing Group)
Stanhope Developments
Surrey County Council
Sustainable Homes
Swaythling Housing Association
    (Radian Group)

Team Pictures
Technology Strategy Board
Telford Homes
Templeton College, Oxford

The Royal Ballet School
Threshold Housing Trust
Tropical Resort Hotels
Turner & Newall

United Reformed Church Trust
    (Southern Province)

Vale of Aylesbury Housing Trust

Wandle Housing Association
Wanted Property Company
Welsh Development Agency
Wildfowl and Wetlands Trust
Wildmoor Properties
Willmott Dixon Design and Build
Willmott Dixon Housing
Wimpey Construction
Wimpey Homes
Wolseley UK
Worcestershire County Council

Credits

ECD Architects

Studio 3
Blue Lion Place
237 Long Lane
London SE1 4PU

tel   +44 (0)20 7939 7500
fax   +44 (0)20 7939 7501
email   ecda@ecda.co.uk
www.ecda.co.uk

Watermark Publications (UK) Limited

PO Box 92
Haslemere
Surrey GU27 2YQ
UK

tel   44 (0)1428 64 3077
fax   44 (0)1428 64 4702
email   ianlambotbooks@aol.com
www.watermarkpublications.com

Designed and edited by Ian Lambot
Text © ECD Architects Ltd

First published in the UK in September 2010
Copyright © 2010 Watermark Publications (UK) Limited
Colour Separations by Evergreen Colour Separation
(Scanning) Co Ltd, Hong Kong
Printed in China by Everbest Printing Company Ltd,
Hong Kong

ISBN 978-1-873200-71-1

Photographs

Building Magazine   10 *(1)*
Clive Boursnell   72 *(1)*
Peter Cook   cover 33 *(1)* 66/67 *(1)* 68 *(1)* 69 *(2)* 70 *(1)*
70/71 *(1)* 72 *(2)* 82 *(1)* 97 *(1)* 98 *(3)* 99 *(2)* 100 *(2)* 101 *(1)*
102 *(2)* 103 *(2)*
Countryside Properties   73 *(1)* 107 *(1)* 108 *(1)* 109 *(1)*
John Donat   12 *(1)* 18 *(1)* 22 *(1)* 23 *(2)*
Richard Ferraro   8 *(2)*
Martine Hamilton-Knight   33 *(2)* 38 *(1)* 44 *(1)* 59 *(2)* 60/61 *(1)*
Nicholas Kane   2 *(1)* 32 *(3)* 33 *(2)* 36 *(1)* 40 *(2)* 50 *(3)* 51 *(2)*
Charles Knevitt   10 *(1)*
Lance McNulty   72 *(1)* 85 *(2)*
Dominic Michaelis   7 *(1)*
Nina Michaelis   6 *(1)*
Ray Merrington   13 *(1)* 32 *(2)* 39 *(1)* 42 *(1)* 48 *(1)* 49 *(2)*
Paul Rafferty   32 *(1)* 39 *(1)*
Nigel Rigden   81 *(1)*
David Turrent   12 *(1)* 18 *(1)* 21 *(1)* 32 *(1)* 40 *(1)* 72 *(1)* 74 *(1)*
79 *(1)* 80 *(1)* 105 *(2)* 118 *(1)*
Paul Tyagi   33 *(4)* 36 *(1)* 37 *(1)* 43 *(1)* 44 *(1)* 56 *(1)* 57 *(1)* 62 *(1)*
63 *(1)* 64 *(2)* 65 *(1)* 72 *(2)* 85 *(1)* 92 *(2)* 92/93 *(1)* 93 *(1)*
Tim Soar   73 *(1)* 111 *(1)* 112 *(1)* 113 *(3)*
Morley von Sternberg   33 *(1)* 83 *(2)*
Tony Weller   12 *(1)* 13 *(2)* 18 *(1)* 24 *(1)* 25 *(1)* 26 *(1)* 27 *(1)* 28 *(1)*
30 *(2)* 31 *(2)* 32 *(1)*

Drawings

Adriette Myburgh   75 *(2)* 76 *(2)* 77 *(1)* 82 *(1)* 90 *(2)* 91 *(1)*
95 *(1)* 104 *(1)* 108 *(1)* 109 *(1)*

Every effort has been made to trace the photographers of all the images used in this book, but those of some of the smaller reference images have eluded us. If you have any further information, please contact the publishers at the address above.